The Definitive Guitar Songbook

ISBN 0-634-02192-3

HAL•LEONARD®
CORPORATION

7777 W. BLUEMOUND RD. P.O. BOX 13819 MILWAUKEE, WI 53213

Visit Hal Leonard Online at
www.halleonard.com

The Definitive Guitar Songbook

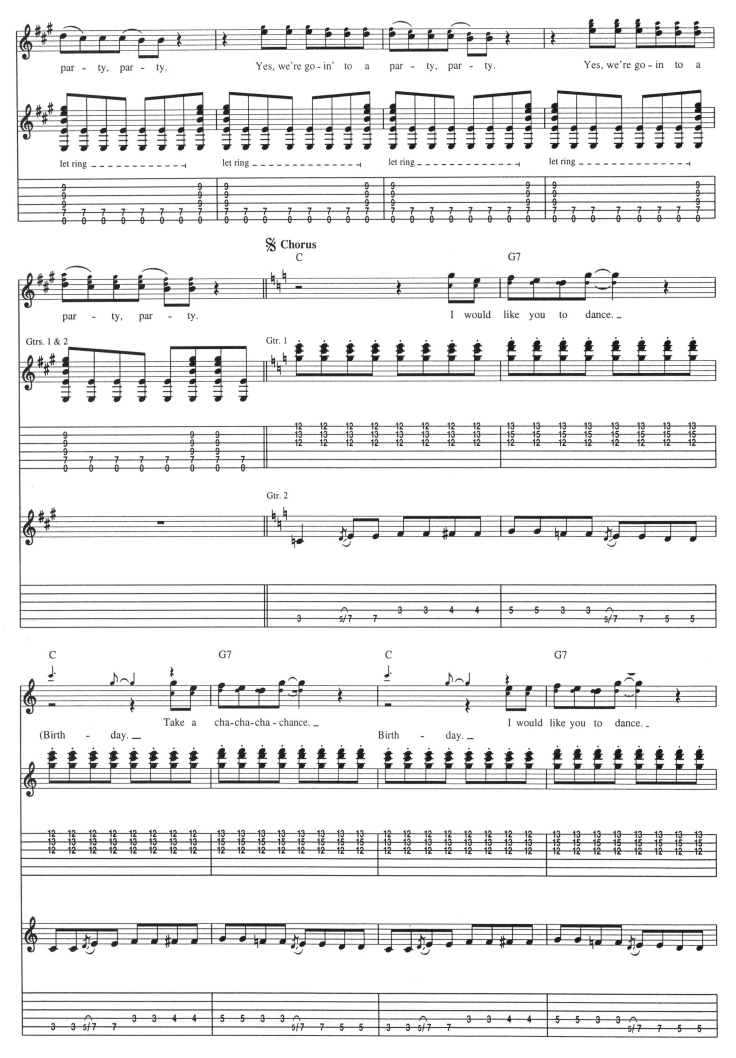

Chorus

6

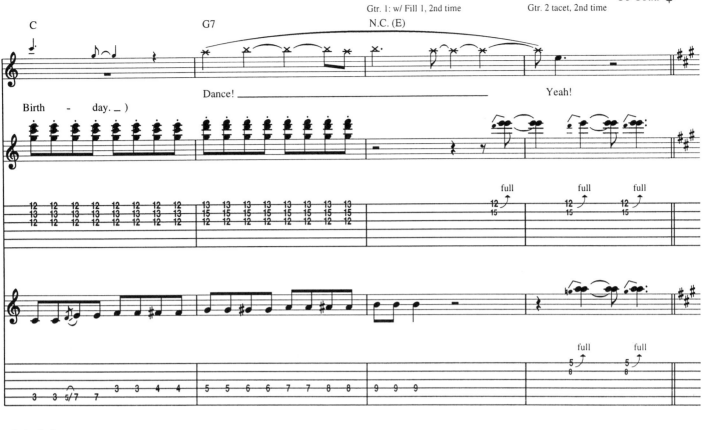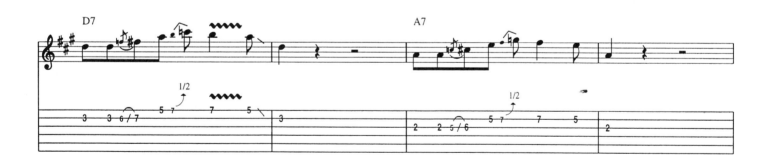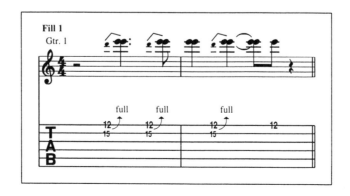

Bulls on Parade

Written and Arranged by Rage Against The Machine

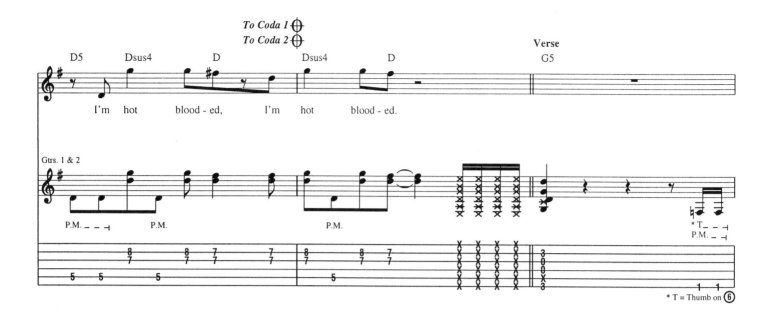

To Coda 1 ⊕
To Coda 2 ⊕

I'm hot blood-ed, I'm hot blood-ed.

1. You don't have to read my mind ___ to know what ___ I

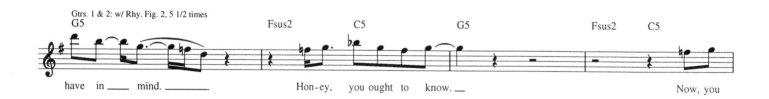

have in ___ mind. ___ Hon-ey, you ought to know. ___ Now, you

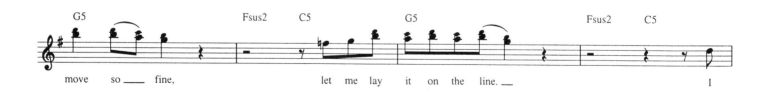

move so ___ fine, let me lay it on the line. ___ I

wan-na know what you're do-in' af-ter the show. ___

14

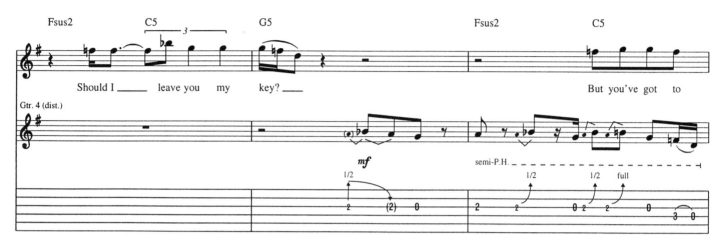

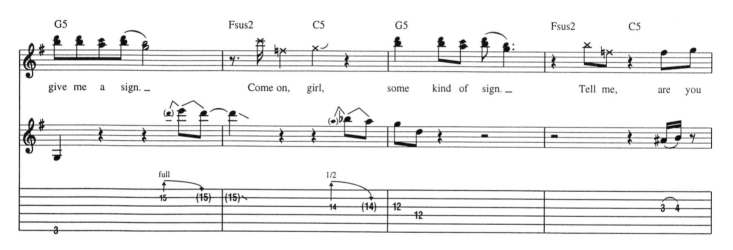

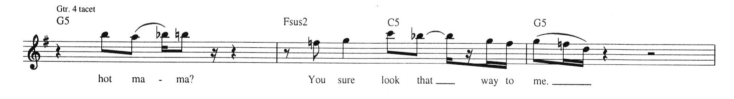

16

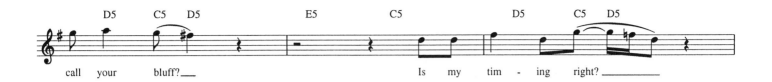

call   your   bluff?___   Is   my   tim - ing   right? _____

D.S. al Coda 2

Gtr. 3: w/ Rhy. Fig. 3, last meas.

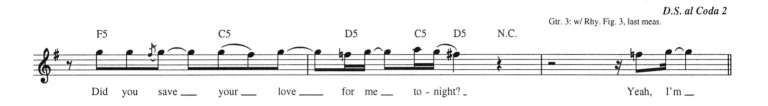

Did   you   save ___   your ___   love ____   for   me ___   to - night? _   Yeah,   I'm ___

⊕ *Coda 2*

Guitar Solo

Gtrs. 1 & 2: w/ Rhy. Fig. 2, 7 1/2 times

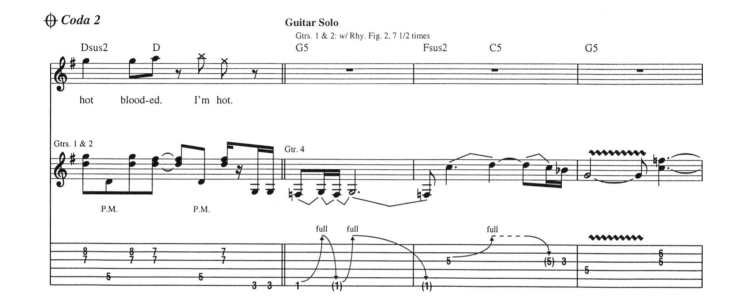

hot   blood-ed.   I'm hot.

pitch: F
* Refers to harm. note only.

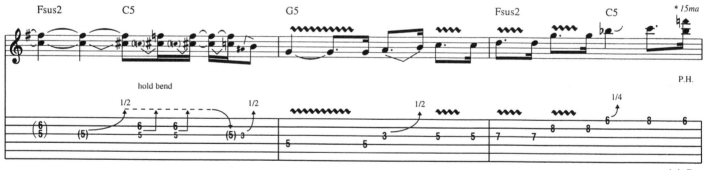

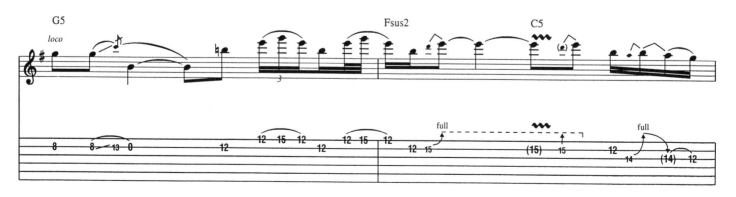

17

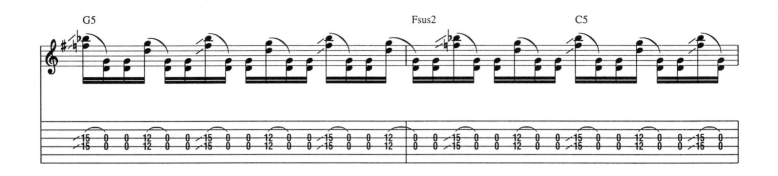

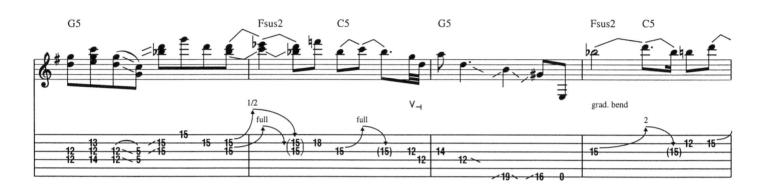

Pre-Chorus
Gtrs. 1 & 2: w/ Rhy. Fig. 3

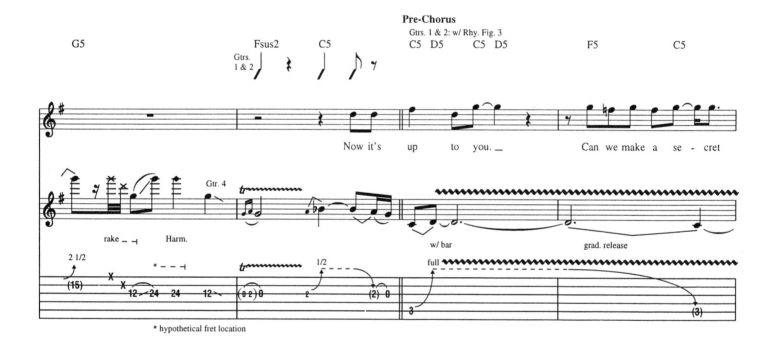

Now it's up to you. ___ Can we make a se - cret

rake ___ Harm.

* hypothetical fret location

ren - dez - vous? ___ Oh. ___ Be - fore we do _____ you'll have to get a - way ___ from

w/ bar

Sto - ry. ____ Grow-ing up ___ in Span-ish Har - lem, ___

she's liv-ing the life ___ just like a mov-ie star. ___ Oh, ___ Ma - ri - a, Ma - ri -

a, ___ *Spoken: Hey you, Maria.* she fell in love ___ in East L. A. ___

to the sounds ___ of a ___ gui - tar, ___ yeah, ___ yeah, ___

Interlude

O-pen up your eyes.) _____

Ma - ri - a, you know you're my lov - er. _____

Gtr. 1

w/ echo — — — — — — — — —   P.M. — — — — — — —

When the wind __ blows I can feel you _____ through __ the weath-

- er. _____ And e - ven when we are a - part _____

it feels __ like we're __ to - geth - er. __ Ma - ri -

she fell in love _____ in East ___ L. A. _____

to the sound _ of a _____ gui - tar

Outro

played by _ Car - los _ San - tan - a.

Spoken: (Put them up, y'all.

Carlos Santana with the refugee gang.

Wyclef,

30

Jerry "Wonder"   *Mr. Santana,*   *G and B.*

Begin fade

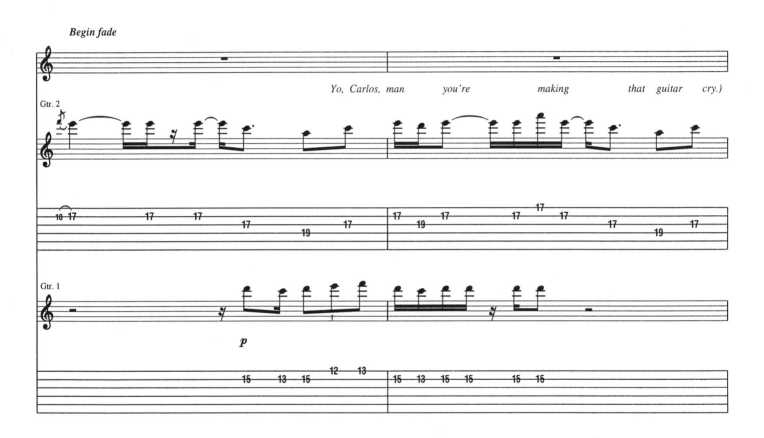

Yo, Carlos, man   you're   making   that guitar   cry.)

Fade out

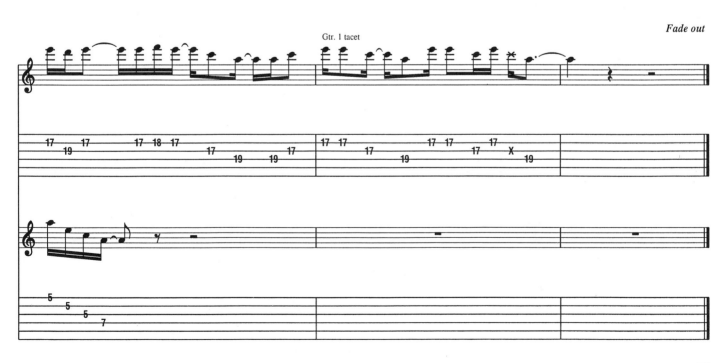

Ramblin' Man

Words and Music by Dickey Betts

*Tune Up 1/2 Step:
① = E#   ④ = D#
② = B#   ⑤ = A#
③ = G#   ⑥ = E#

Intro
Fast Rock ♩ = 184

N.C.(G)   (D)   (C)   (G)

Gtr. 1

Gtr. 2

Gtr. 1

divisi

* or Capo 1   * Gtr. 1 to left of slash in TAB.

Chorus
Gtr. 2 tacet

G   F   C   G

Lord,   I ___ was born ___ a ram - blin' man. ___

Gtr. 1   **Rhy. Fig. 1**

loco

___   C

___ Try'n to make a liv-ing, and do-in' the best I ___

D6   D   C

___ can.   An' when it's time ___ for

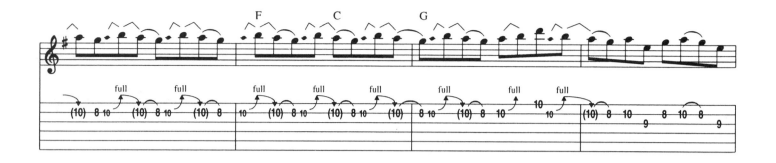

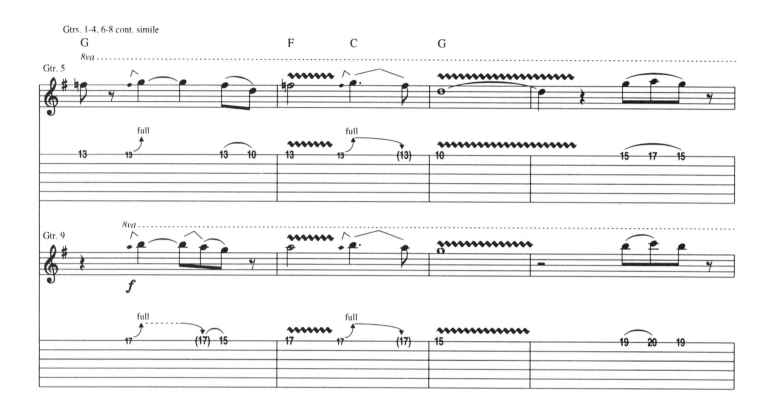

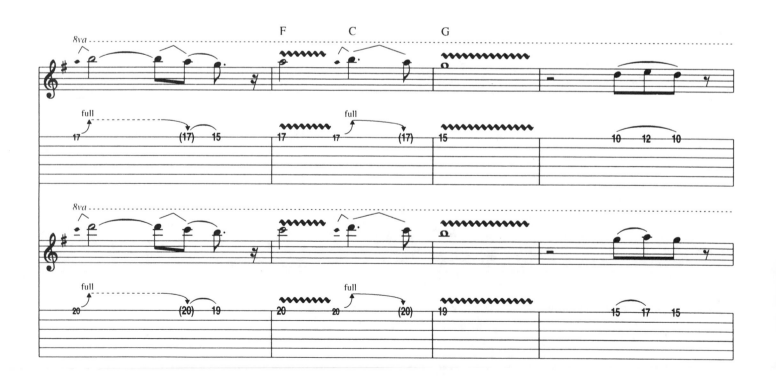

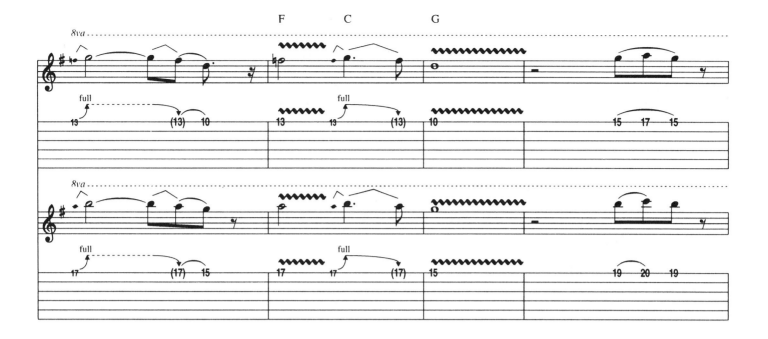

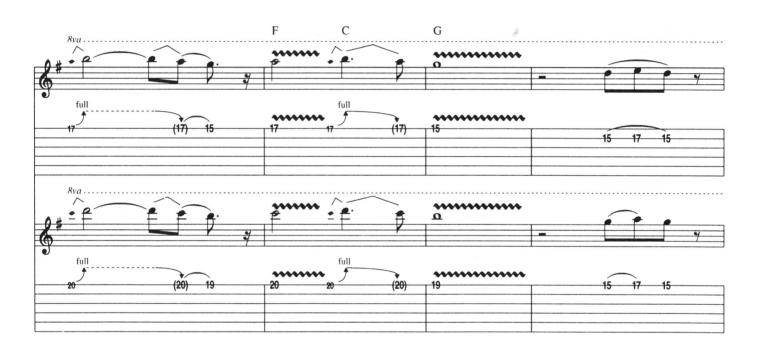

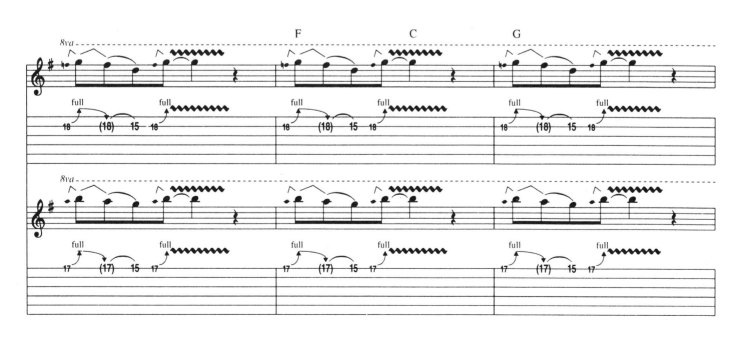

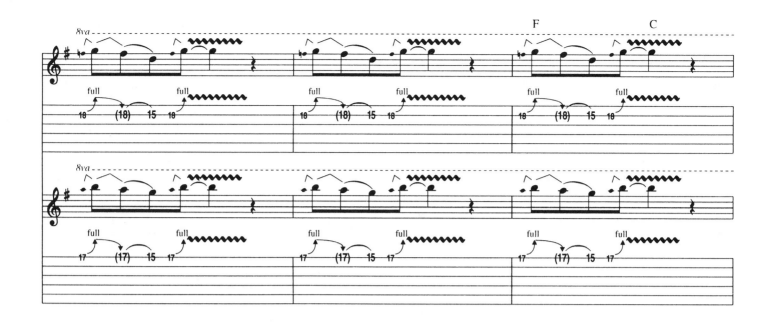

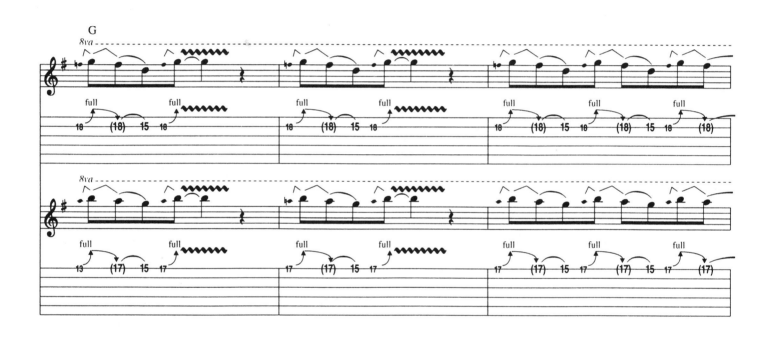

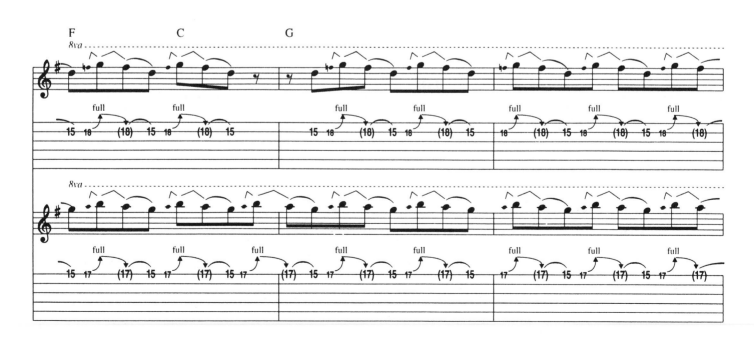

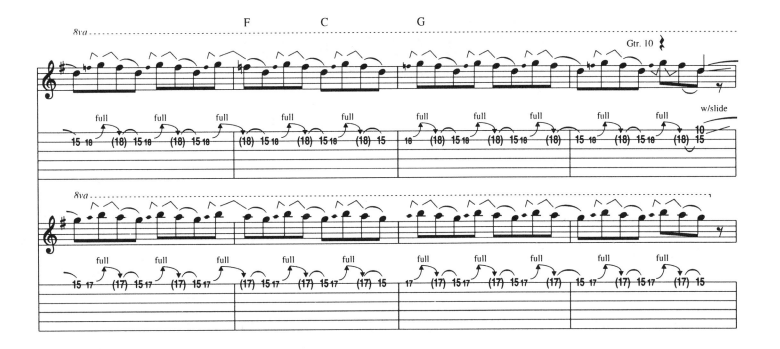

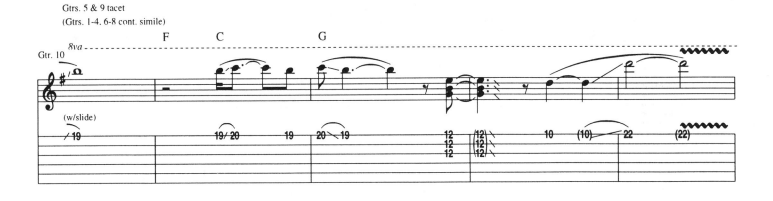

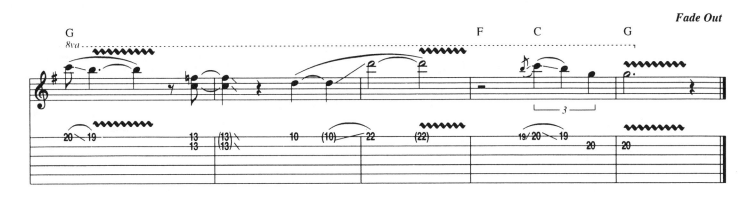

Riding With the King

Words and Music by John Hiatt

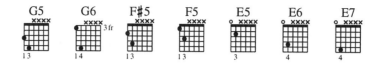

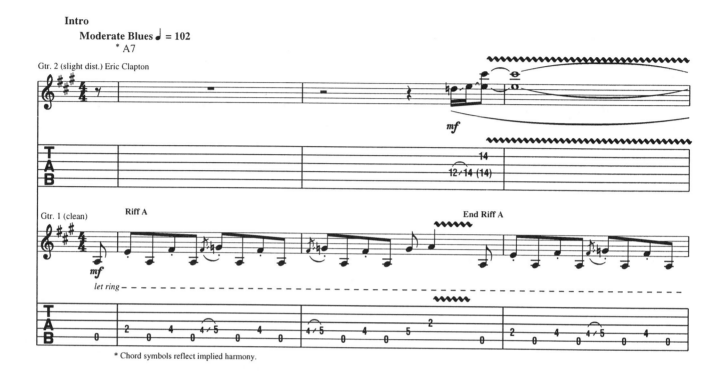

* Chord symbols reflect implied harmony.

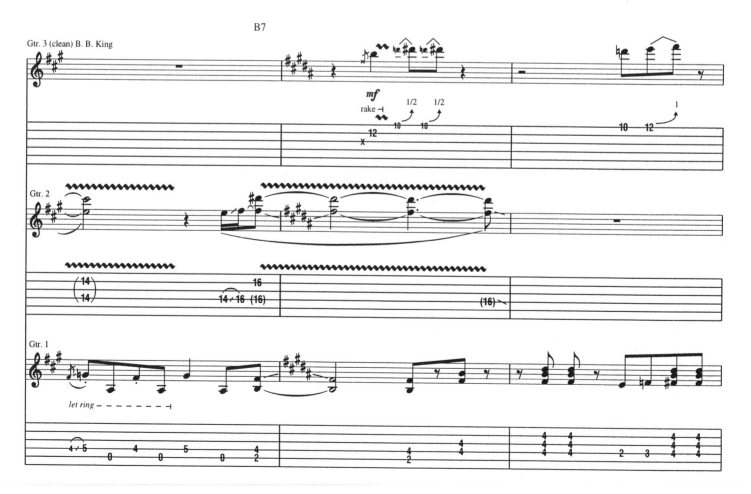

Verse

B7

1. I dreamed I had a good job and I

* Eric Clapton-full size notes, B.B. King-cue size notes.

Gtr. 2 tacet

E7

got well - paid. __ I blew it all at the pen - ny ar - cade.

Gtr. 3

Gtr. 1

* Cue notes are female harmony (next 2 meas.).
  Eric Clapton upstem notes,
  B.B. King downstem notes.

**Eric Clapton-full size notes,
  B.B. King-cue size notes,

46

Verse

Gtr. 1: w/ Rhy. Fig. 1

B7

mis-sion of mer-cy to a new fron - tier. __

He's gon-na check us all out, out of here. __

Gtr. 3

Gtr. 2

E7

B7

Up to that man-sion on { the hill, __ } { on the hill, __ }

Gtr. 3 tacet

E7

where you can get your pre - scrip - tion __ filled _____

B.B. King, Spoken: *Any kind of pill, folks,*

Gtr. 2

King?
King.
Spoken: Yeah, you're ridin' with The King.

We're rid-in' with The   King.

Don't you know you're rid-in' with The
You're rid-in' with The

King?
King.)

Bridge

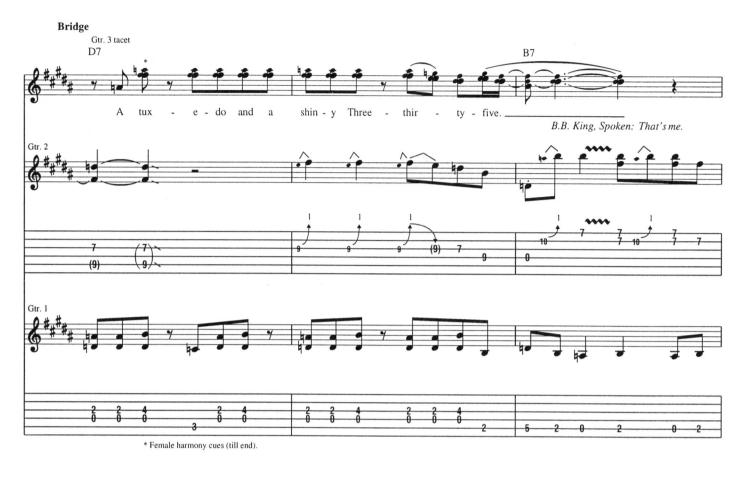

A tux - e - do and a shin - y Three - thir - ty - five. _____

B.B. King, Spoken: That's me.

* Female harmony cues (till end).

You can see it in his face, the blues is his life. __
Ha, ha, ha.

50

Recitation

King? _____

B.B. King, Spoken: I stepped out of Mississippi when I was ten years old,   with a suit cut sharp   as a

razor,   and   a   heart   made   of   gold.   I had a guitar hang-in' just about waist high,

Rhy. Fig. 3

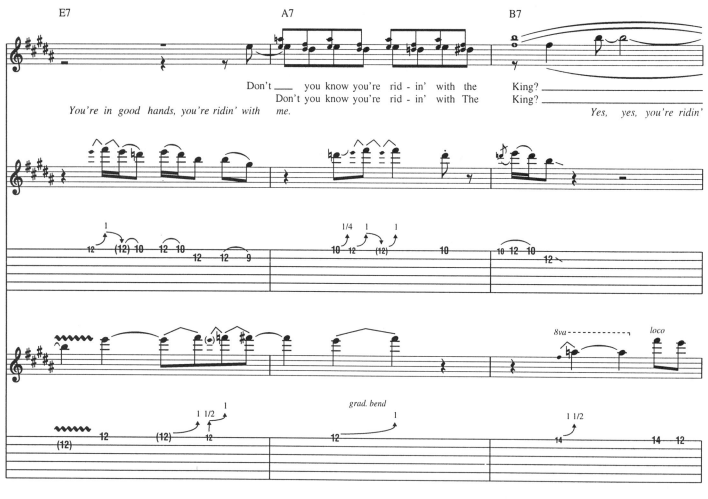

Don't ___ you know you're rid - in' with the King? ___
Don't you know you're rid - in' with The King? ___

You're in good hands, you're ridin' with me.
Yes, yes, you're ridin'

with The King.
I wanted to say B.B. King, but you know who King is.

You're rid - in', you're rid - in' with The
You're rid - in' with The

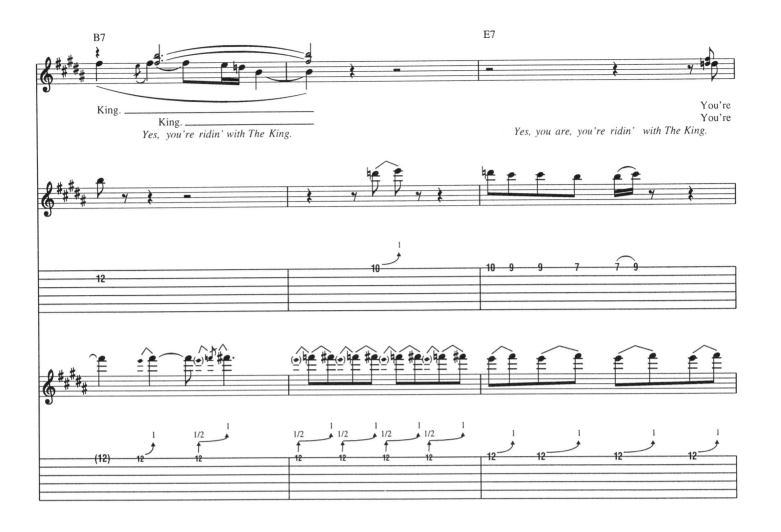

King. _____
     King. _____
Yes, you're ridin' with The King.

You're
You're
Yes, you are, you're ridin' with The King.

rid - in',   you're rid - in'   with The   King. _____
rid - in',   you're rid - in'   with The   King.
You're ridin' with The King.

Rid - in'   with The
I'm a good chauffer too.

Wild World

Words and Music by Cat Stevens

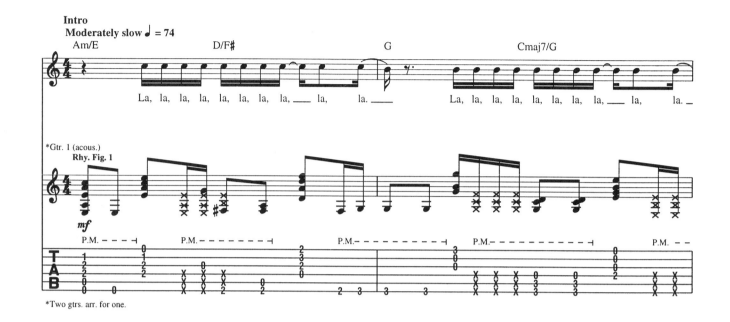

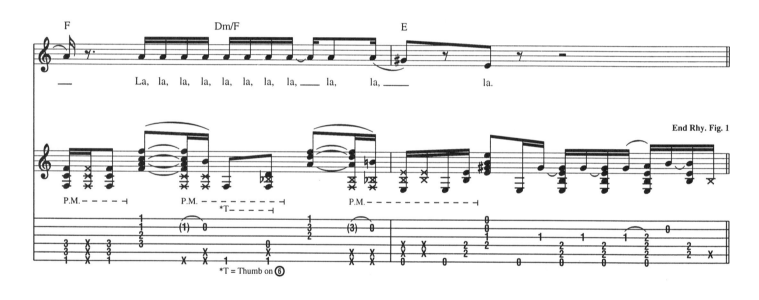

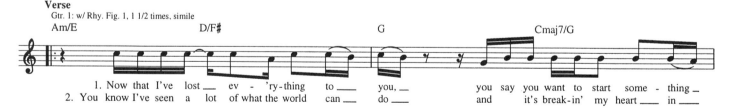

You've Got a Friend

Words and Music by Carole King

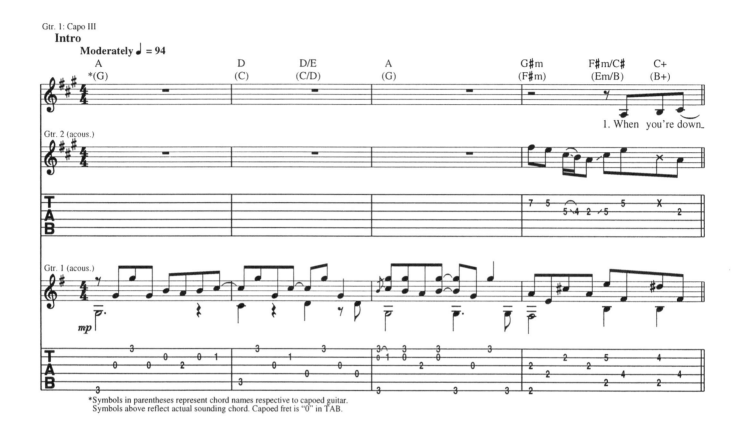

*Symbols in parentheses represent chord names respective to capoed guitar.
Symbols above reflect actual sounding chord. Capoed fret is "0" in TAB.

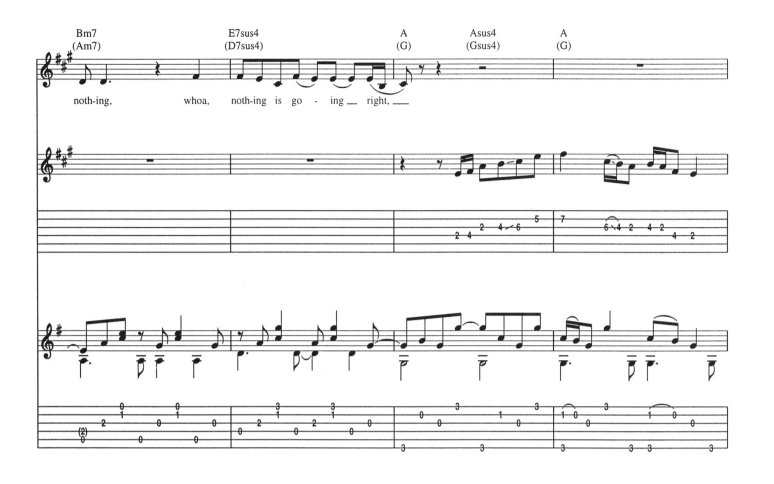

nothing,   whoa,   noth-ing is go - ing __ right,

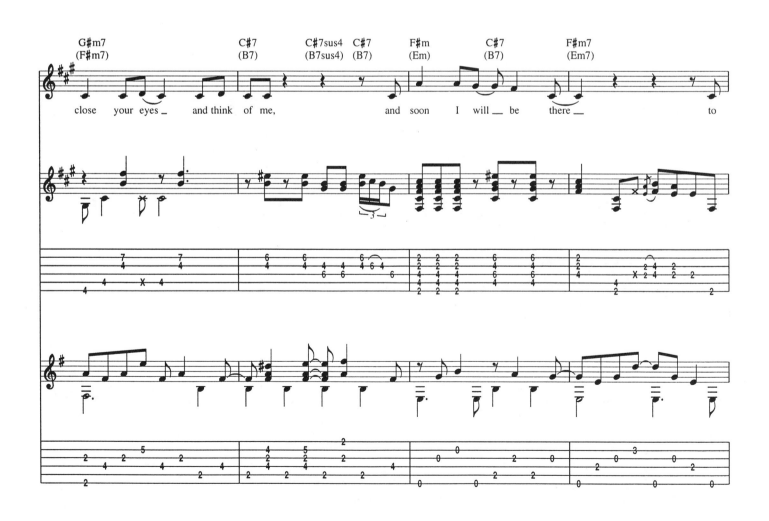

close   your eyes __ and think of me,   and soon I will __ be there __   to

bright-en up   e-ven your dark - est night.   You just call

Chorus

___ out my ___ name, ___   and you know wher-ev - er I am, ___   I'll come run-

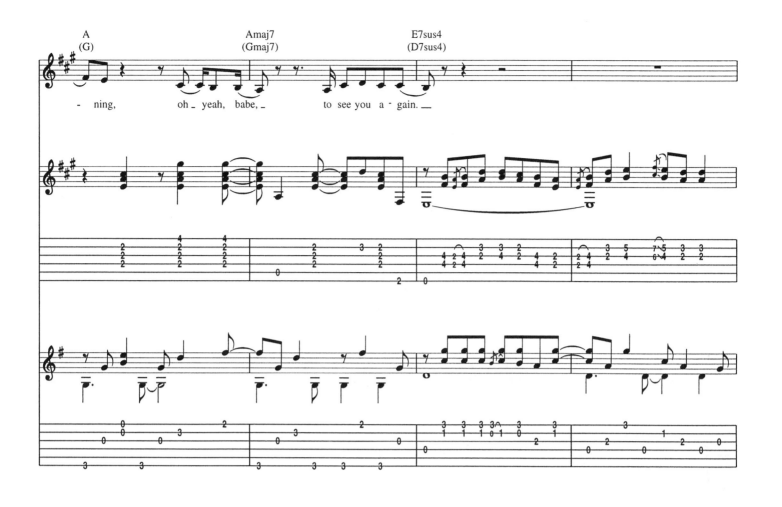

- ning, oh _ yeah, babe, _ to see you a - gain. _

Win-ter, spring, sum-mer or fall, _ now, all you got to do _ is _ call, _ and I'll

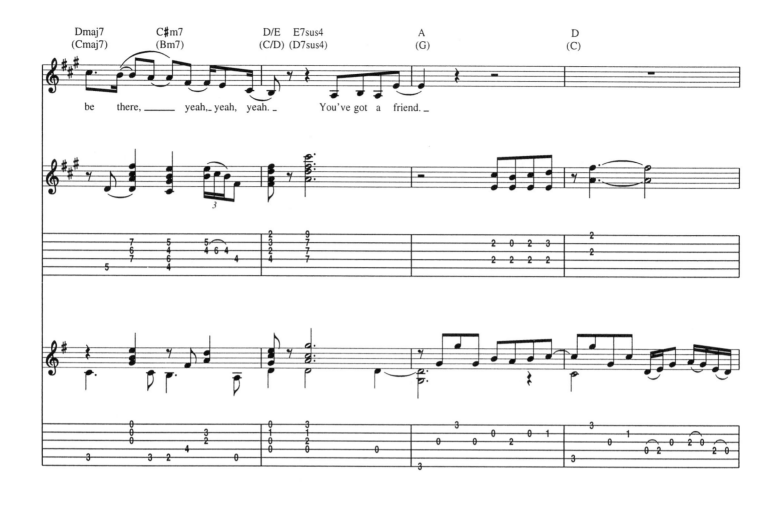

be there, _____ yeah,_ yeah, yeah._ You've got a friend._

Verse

2. If the sky _____ a - bove _ you should turn_

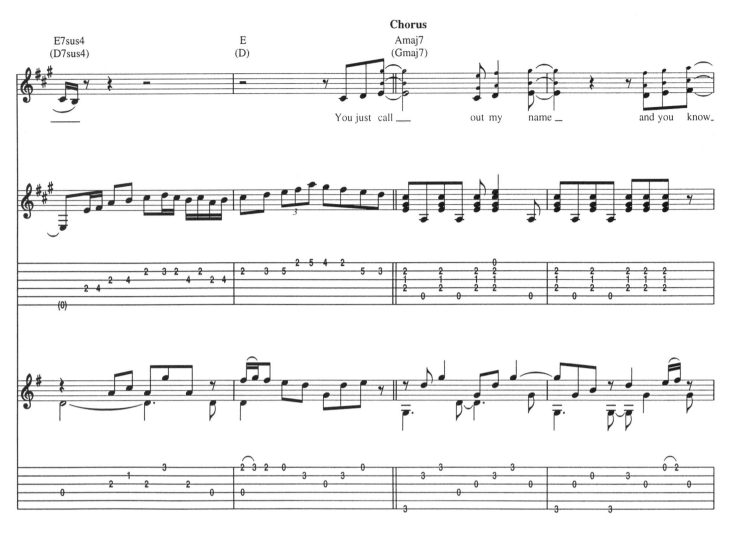

Chorus

You just call ___ out my name ___ and you know ___

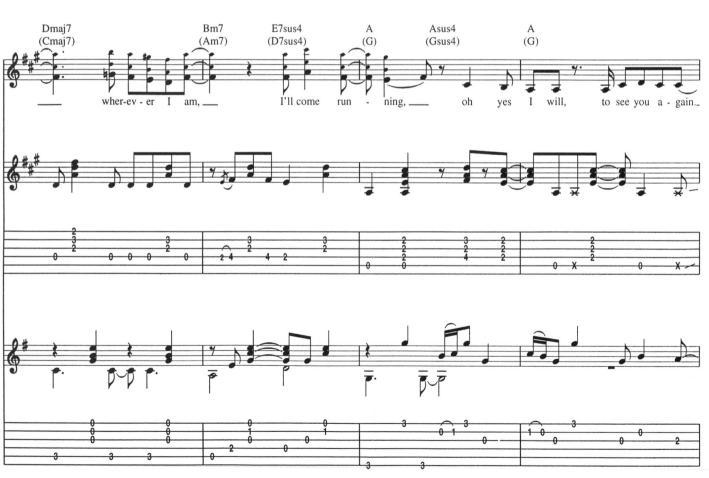

wher-ev-er I am, ___ I'll come run - ning, ___ oh yes I will, to see you a - gain. ___

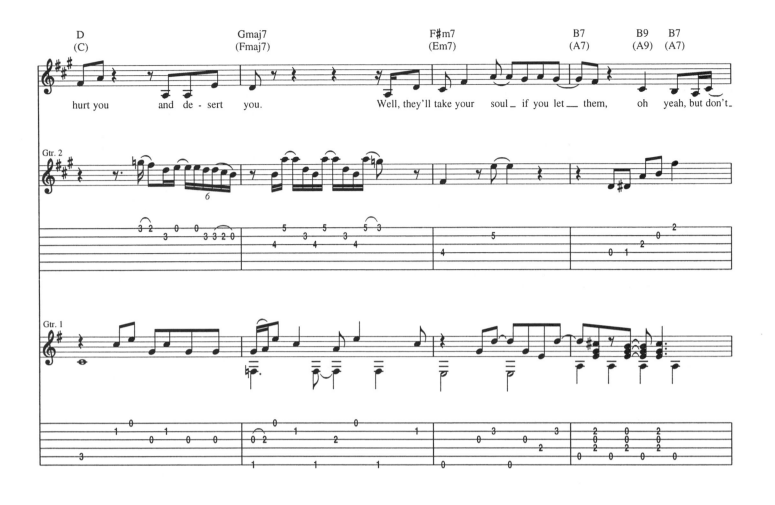

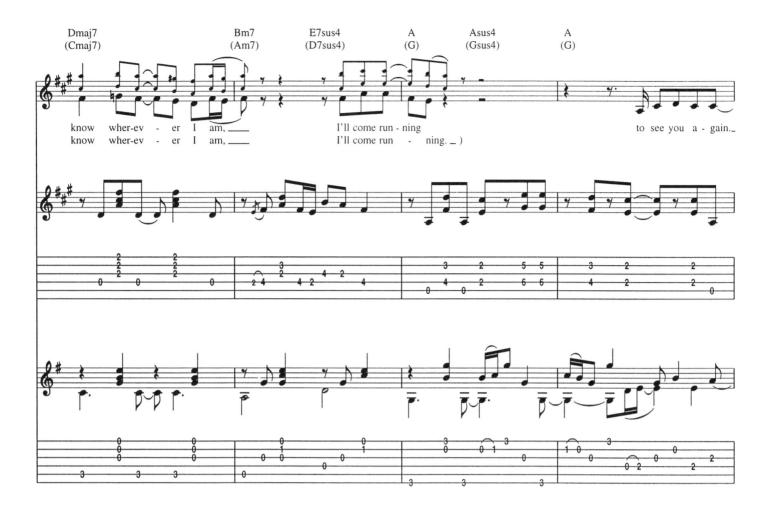

know wher-ev - er I am, ___ I'll come run - ning to see you a - gain. ___

know wher-ev - er I am, ___ I'll come run - ning. ___)

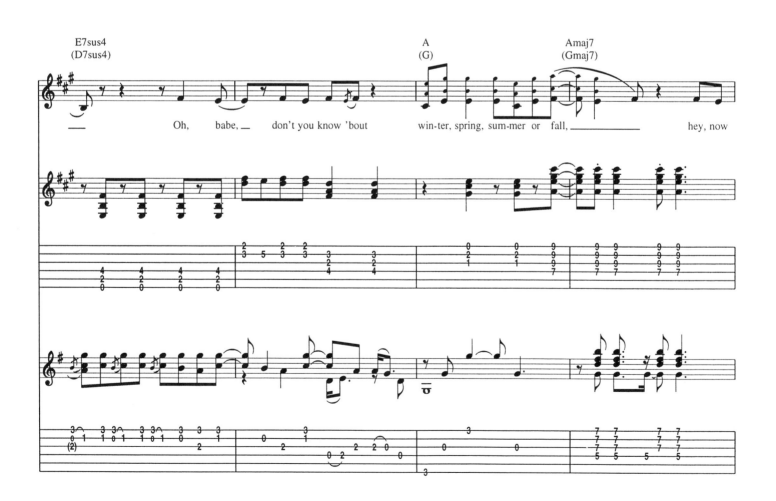

Oh, babe, ___ don't you know 'bout win-ter, spring, sum-mer or fall, ___ hey, now

All I Have to Do Is Dream

Words and Music by Boudleaux Bryant

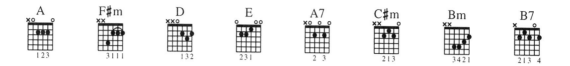

Strum Pattern: 3
Pick Pattern: 3

Intro
Moderately

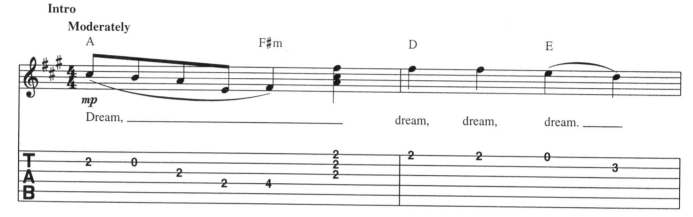

Dream, _____ dream, dream, dream. _____

Dream, _____ dream, dream, dream. _____ 1. When

I want you _____ in my arms, when I want you _____
2. *See Additional Lyrics*

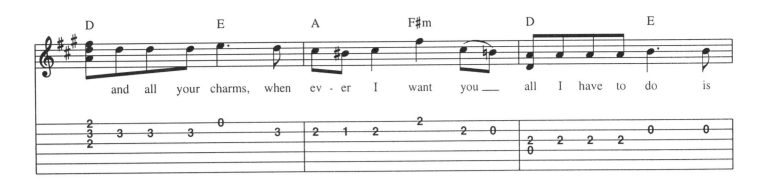

and all your charms, when ev-er I want you ___ all I have to do is

dream, ___ dream, dream, dream. 2.When dream. ___

Bridge

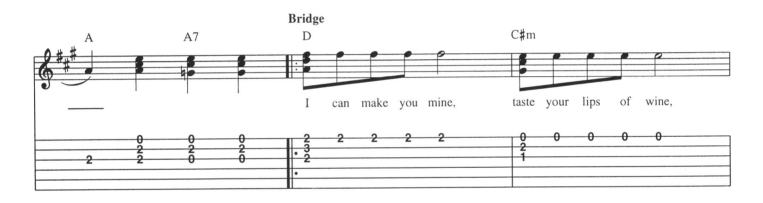

___ I can make you mine, taste your lips of wine,

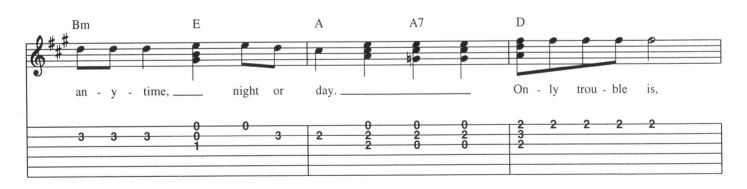

an-y-time, ___ night or day. ___ On-ly trou-ble is,

gee whiz, I'm dream-ing my life ___ a-way. ___ 3., 4. I

Barely Breathing

Words and Music by Duncan Sheik

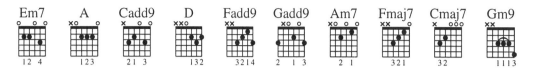

Em7 A Cadd9 D Fadd9 Gadd9 Am7 Fmaj7 Cmaj7 Gm9

Strum Pattern: 1
Pick Pattern: 2

Intro
Moderately

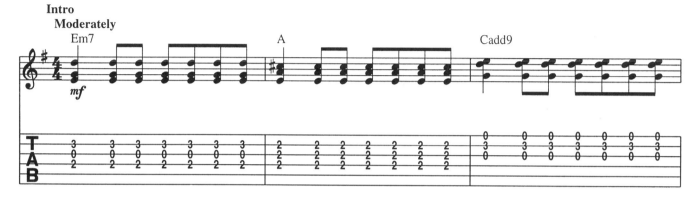

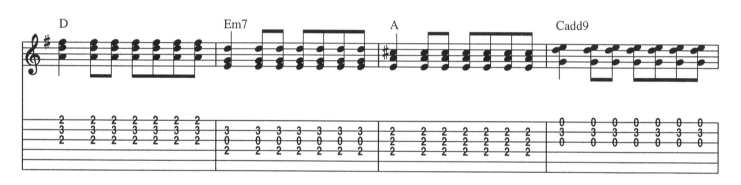

Verse

1. Well, I know what you're do-ing. I see it all too clear. I on-ly taste the

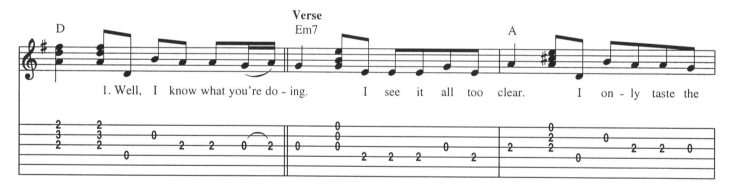

sa-line when I kiss a-way your tears. You real-ly had me go-ing, wish-ing on a

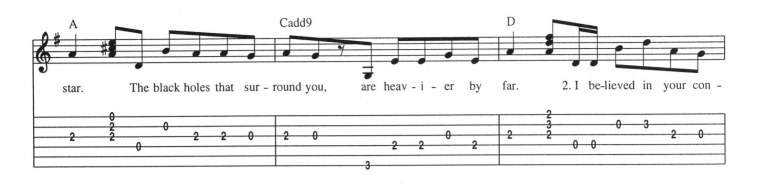

star. The black holes that sur- round you, are heav- i- er by far. 2. I be-lieved in your con-

Verse

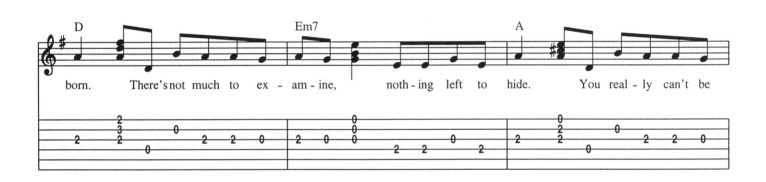

fu- sion, so com-plete-ly torn. __ It must have been that yes-ter-day ____ was the day that I was
3. *See Additional Lyrics*

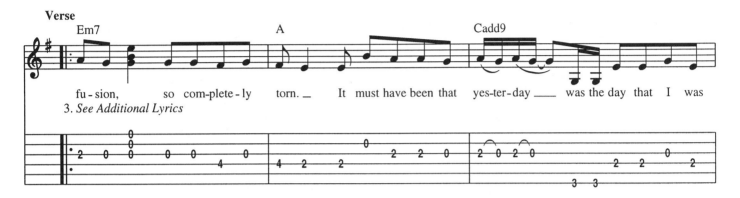

born. There's not much to ex- am- ine, noth- ing left to hide. You real- ly can't be

se- ri- ous, you have to ask me why I say _____ good - bye. _____

𝄋 Chorus

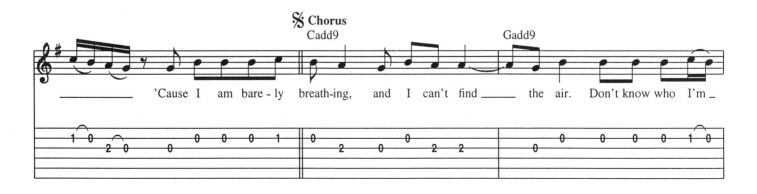

_____ ____ 'Cause I am bare- ly breath-ing, and I can't find _____ the air. Don't know who I'm _

Additional Lyrics

3. And ev'ryone keeps asking what's it all about.
   It used to be so certain. Now I can't figure out.
   What is this attraction? Don't it fill the day,
   And nothing left to reason, and only you to blame.
   Will it ever change?

Big City

Words and Music by Merle Haggard and Dean Holloway

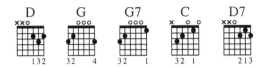

Strum Pattern: 4, 6
Pick Pattern: 3, 4

Intro
Reflectively

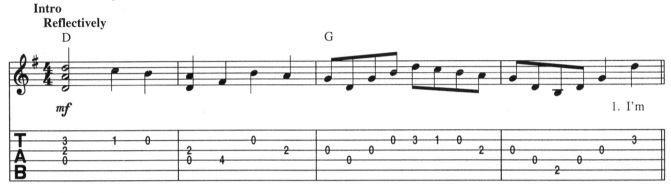

1. I'm

Verse

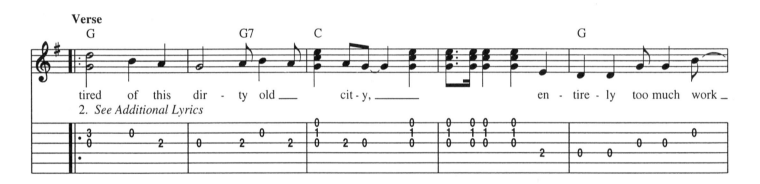

tired of this dir - ty old ___ cit - y, ___ en - tire - ly too much work ___
2. *See Additional Lyrics*

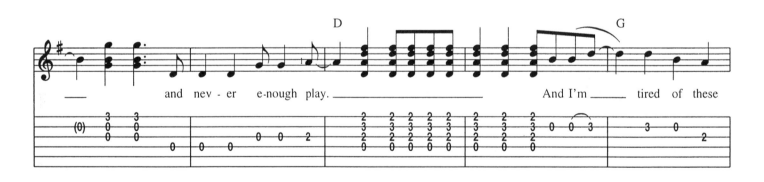

___ and nev - er e - nough play. ___ And I'm ___ tired of these

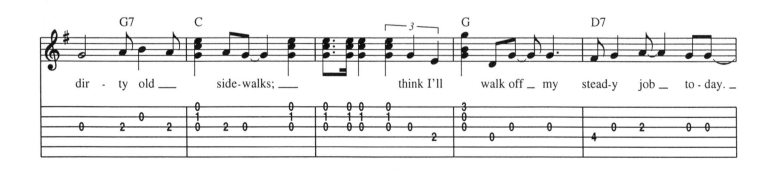

dir - ty old ___ side - walks; ___ think I'll walk off ___ my stead - y job to - day. ___

Chorus

Turn me loose, set me free, _____ some-where in the

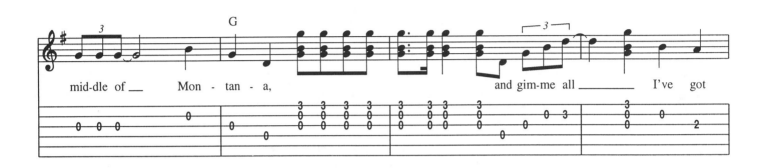

mid-dle of __ Mon - tan - a, and gim-me all _____ I've got

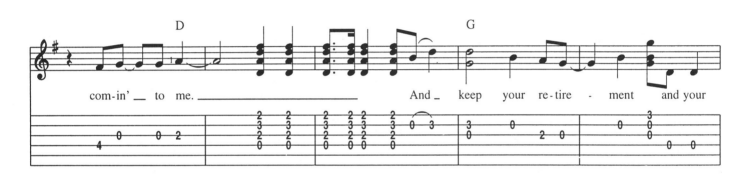

com-in' __ to me. _____ And _ keep your re-tire - ment and your

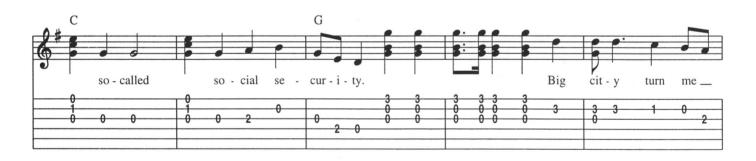

so - called so - cial se - cur - i - ty. Big cit - y turn me __

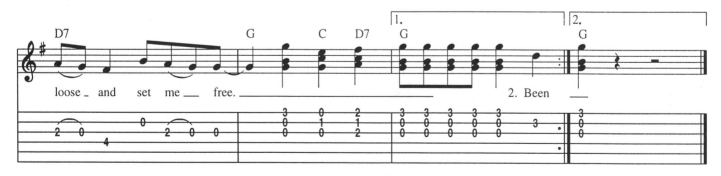

loose _ and set me _ free. _____ 2. Been __

Additional Lyrics

2. Been workin' ev'ryday since I was twenty,
Haven't got a thing to show for anything I've done.
There's folks who never work and they've got plenty;
Think it's time some guys like me had some fun.

Blackbird

Words and Music by John Lennon and Paul McCartney

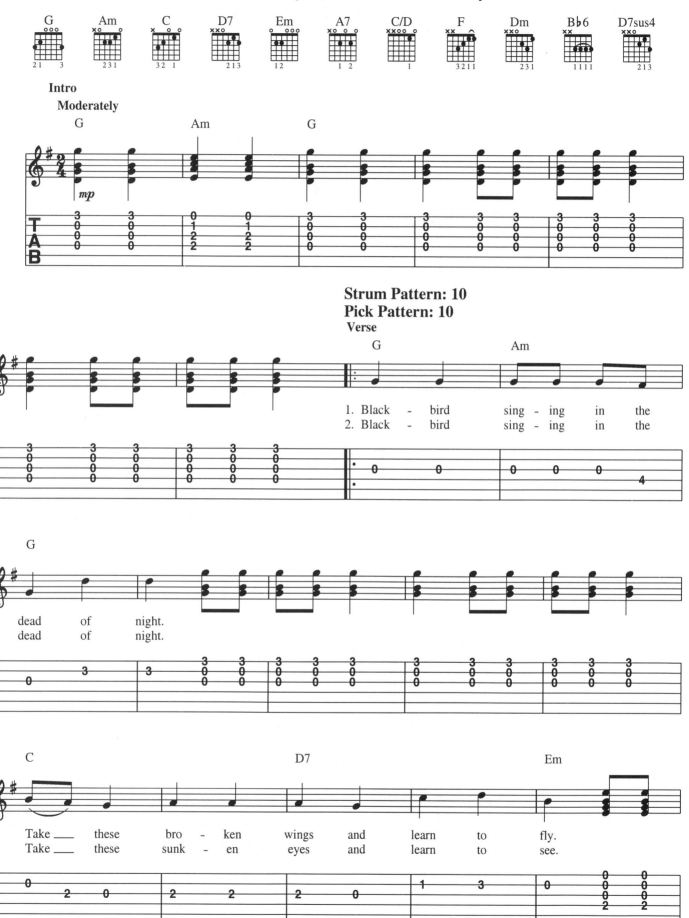

Strum Pattern: 10
Pick Pattern: 10

Verse

1. Black - bird sing - ing in the
2. Black - bird sing - ing in the

dead of night.
dead of night.

Take ___ these bro - ken wings and learn to fly.
Take ___ these sunk - en eyes and learn to see.

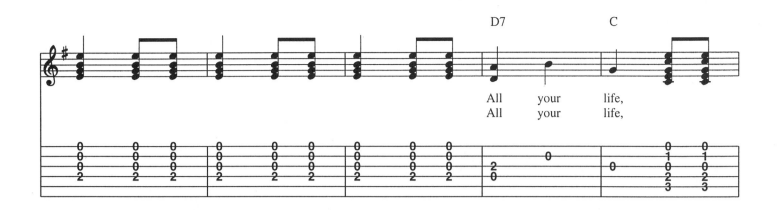

All your life,
All your life,

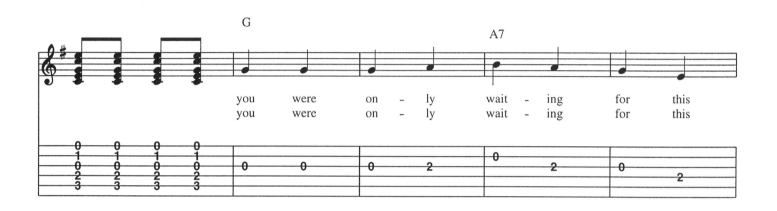

you were on – ly wait – ing for this
you were on – ly wait – ing for this

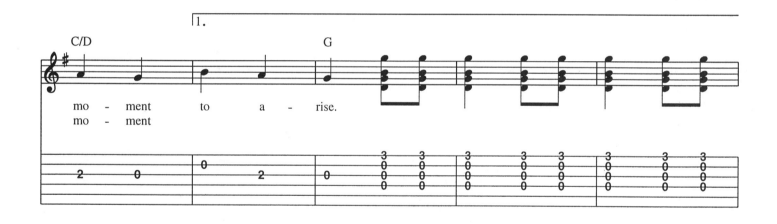

mo – ment to a – rise.
mo – ment

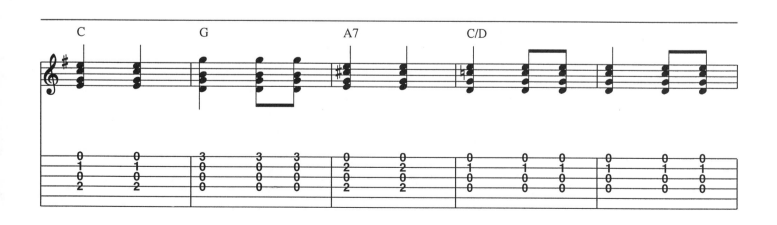

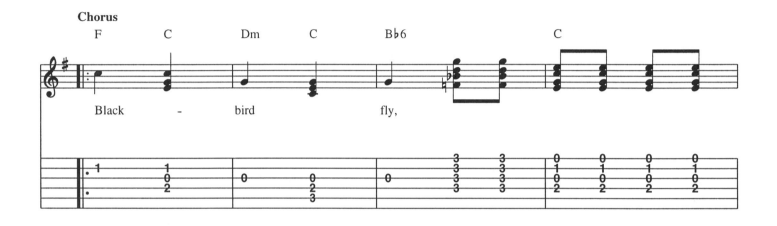

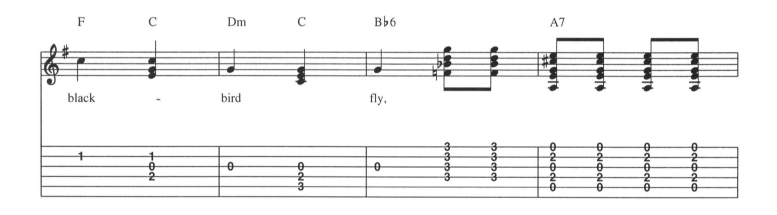

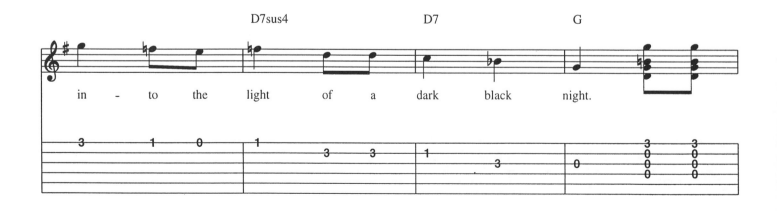

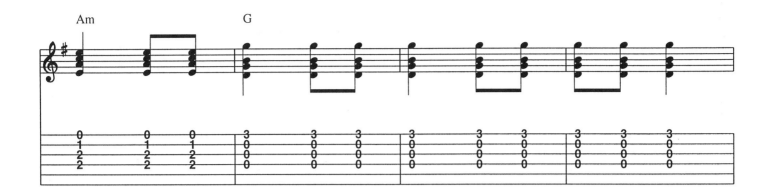

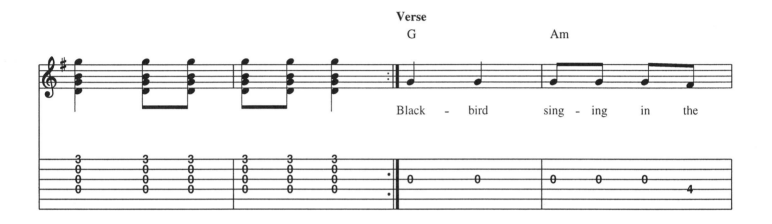

Black - bird sing - ing in the

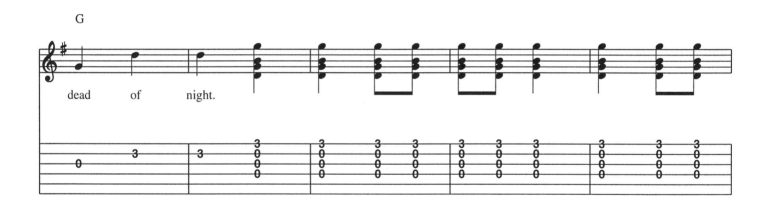

dead of night.

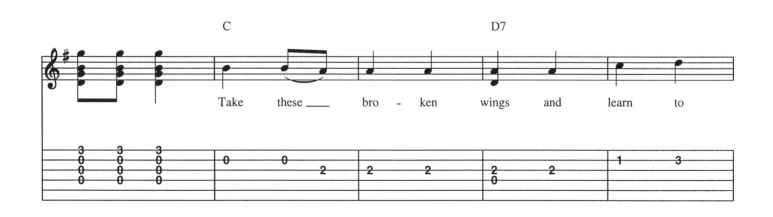

Take these ___ bro - ken wings and learn to

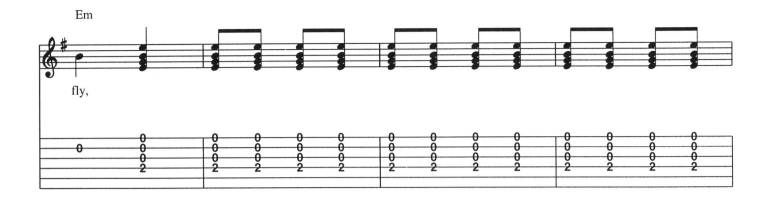

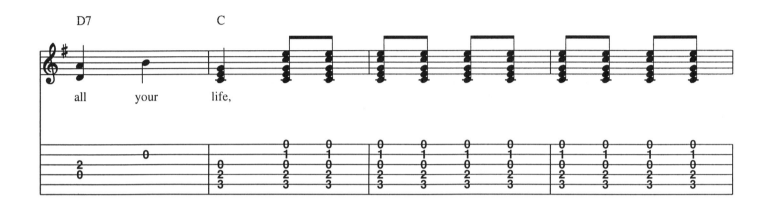

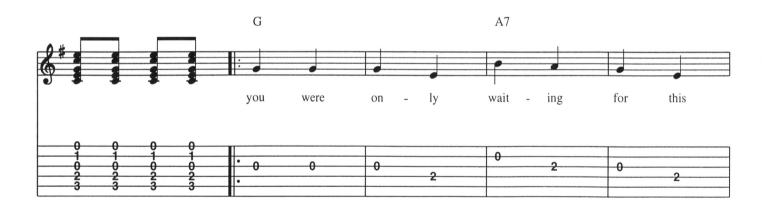

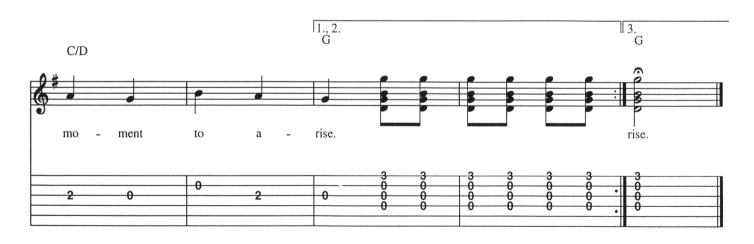

Crossfire

Written by Bill Carter, Ruth Ellsworth, Reese Wynans, Tommy Shannon and Chris Layton

Boom Boom

By John Lee Hooker

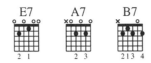

Strum Pattern: 2, 3
Pick Pattern: 2, 4

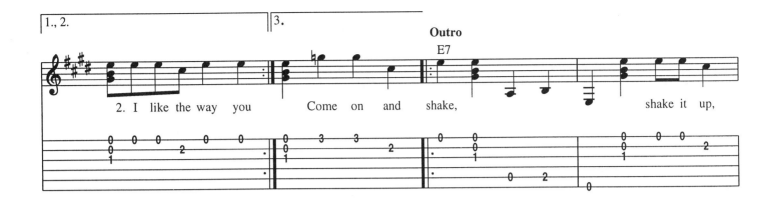

2. I like the way you | Come on and shake, | shake it up,

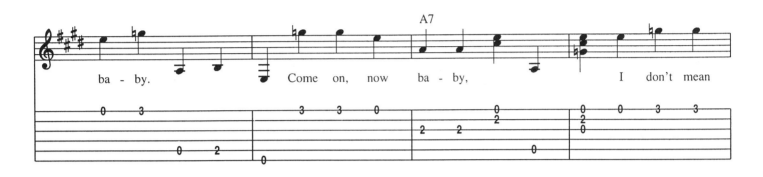

ba - by. | Come on, now ba - by, | I don't mean

may - be. _____ | You're driv-in' me cra - zy, come on, come
                  | Come on, _ come on, _____ all right, all

on. | Come on and right. | right.

Additional Lyrics

2. I like the way you walk.
   I like the way you talk.
   When you walk that walk,
   And when you talk that talk,
   You knock me out,
   Right off my feet.

3. I need you right now,
   I mean right now.
   I don't mean tomorrow,
   I mean right now.
   Come on, come on,
   Come shake it up, baby.

Do-Re-Mi

from THE SOUND OF MUSIC

Lyrics by Oscar Hammerstein II
Music by Richard Rodgers

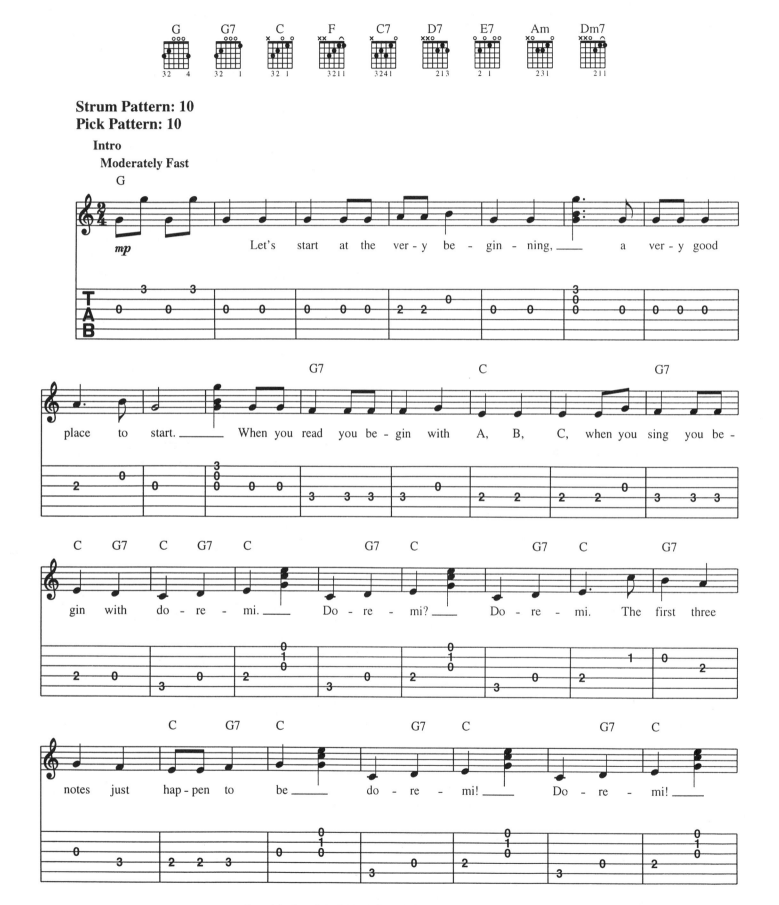

Strum Pattern: 10
Pick Pattern: 10

Intro
Moderately Fast

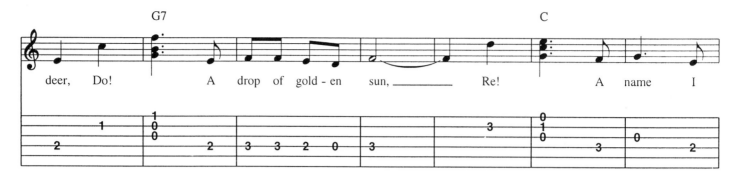

deer, Do! A drop of gold - en sun, _____ Re! A name I

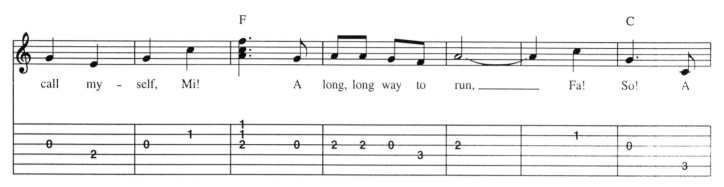

call my - self, Mi! A long, long way to run, _____ Fa! So! A

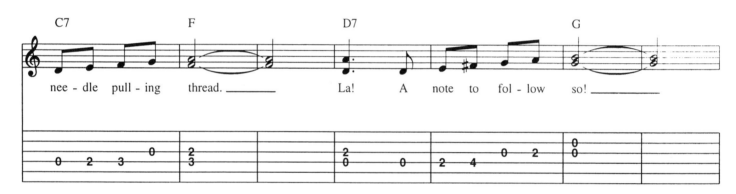

nee - dle pull - ing thread. _____ La! A note to fol - low so! _____

D.S. al Coda

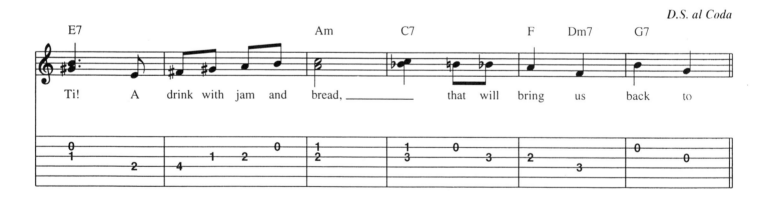

Ti! A drink with jam and bread, _____ that will bring us back to

✛ *Coda*

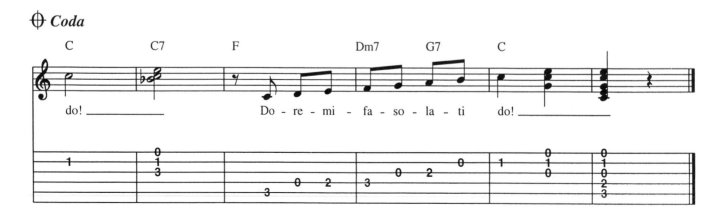

do! _____ Do - re - mi - fa - so - la - ti do! _____

Don't Be Cruel
(To a Heart That's True)

Words and Music by Otis Blackwell and Elvis Presley

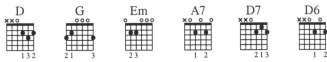

Strum Pattern: 3, 4
Pick Pattern: 3, 5

Intro
Medium Bright Shuffle Feel

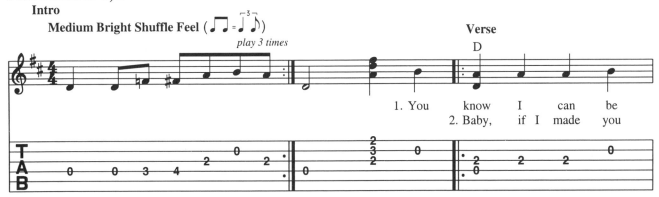

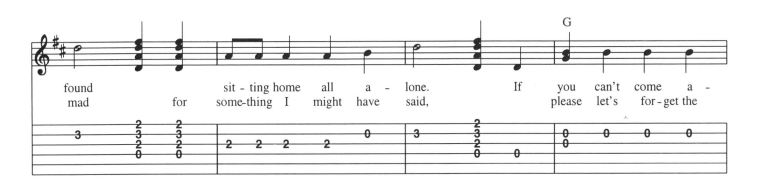

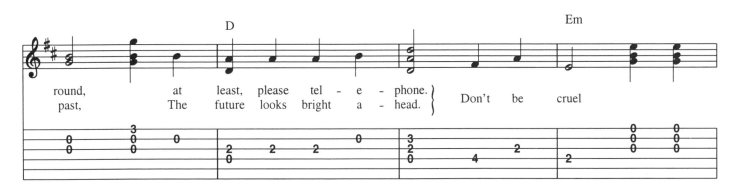

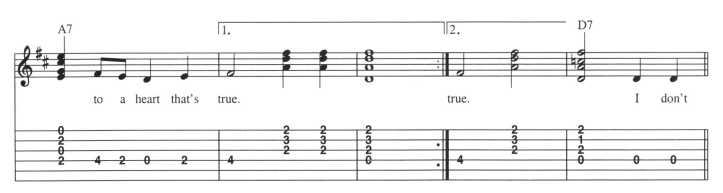

Frosty the Snow Man

Words and Music by Steve Nelson and Jack Rollins

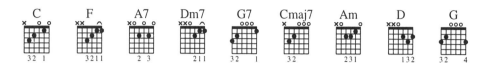

Strum Pattern: 2, 3
Pick Pattern: 3, 4

Verse
Moderately Fast

1. Frost - y the snow man was a jol - ly hap - py
3. *See Additional Lyrics*

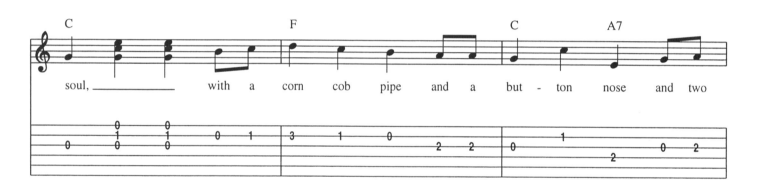

soul, _____ with a corn cob pipe and a but - ton nose and two

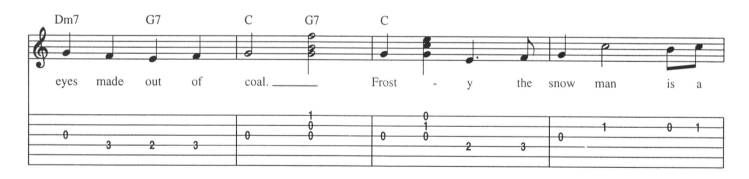

eyes made out of coal. _____ Frost - y the snow man is a

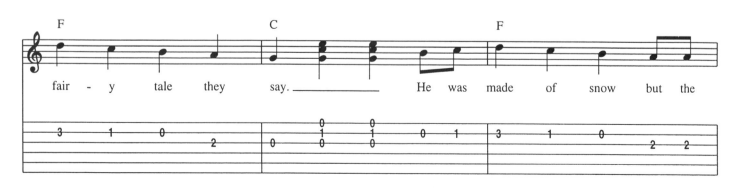

fair - y tale they say. _____ He was made of snow but the

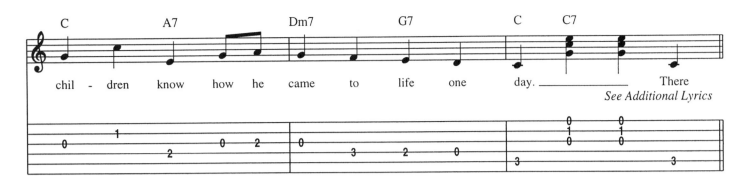

chil - dren know how he came to life one day. _____ There
See Additional Lyrics

Bridge

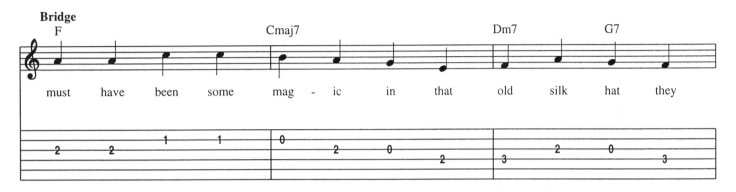

must have been some mag - ic in that old silk hat they

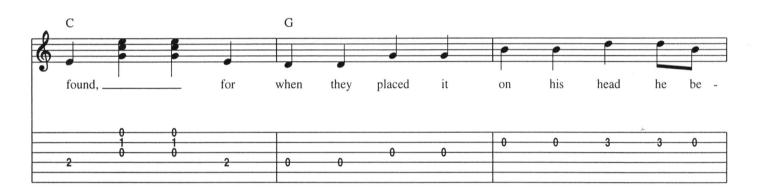

found, _____ for when they placed it on his head he be -

Verse

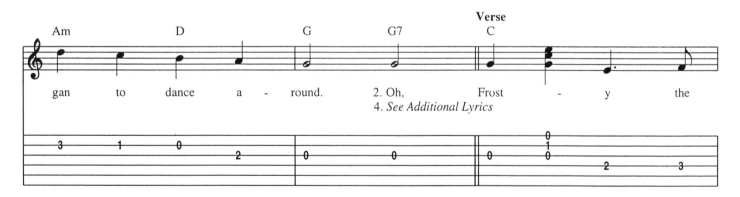

gan to dance a - round. 2. Oh, Frost - y the
4. *See Additional Lyrics*

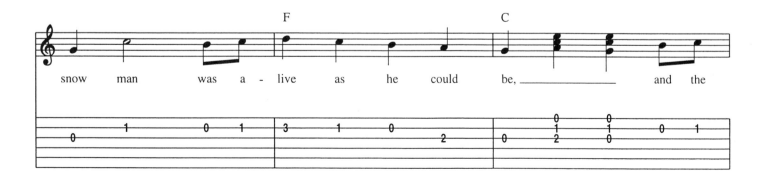

snow man was a - live as he could be, _____ and the

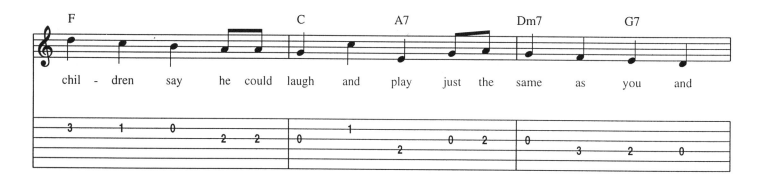

chil - dren say he could laugh and play just the same as you and

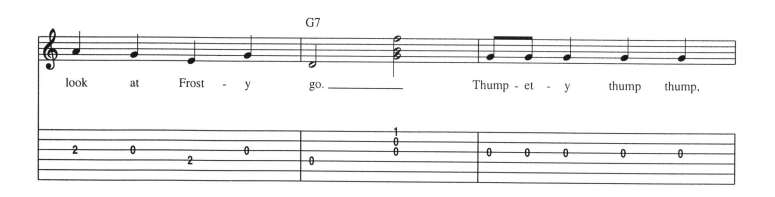

Outro

me. _____ Thump - et - y thump thump, thump - et - y thump thump,

look at Frost - y go. _____ Thump - et - y thump thump,

thump - et - y thump thump, o - ver the hills of snow. _____

Additional Lyrics

3. Frosty the snowman knew the sun was hot that day,
   So he said, "Let's run and we'll have some fun now before I melt away."
   Down to the village with a broomstick in his hand,
   Running here and there and all around the square, sayin', "Catch me if you can."

Bridge: He led them down the streets of town right to the traffic cop,
   And he only paused a moment when he heard him holler, "Stop!"

4. For Frosty the snowman had to hurry on his way,
   But he waved goodbye sayin', "Don't you cry, I'll be back again someday."

I Heard It Through the Grapevine

Words and Music by Norman J. Whitfield and Barrett Strong

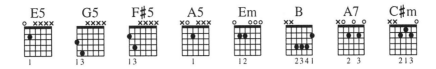

Strum Pattern: 3
Pick Pattern: 3

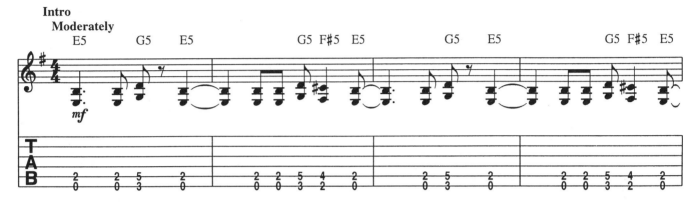

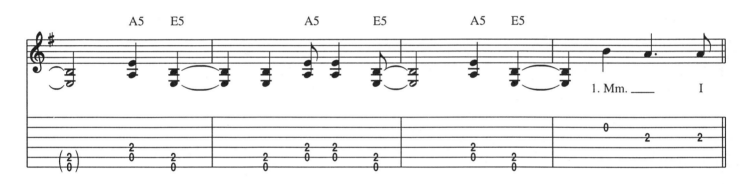

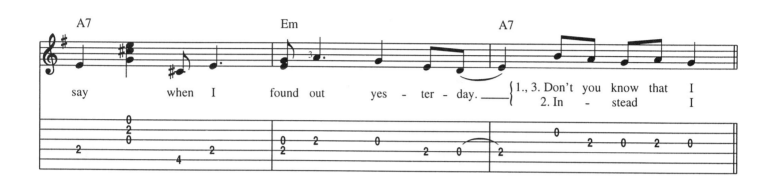

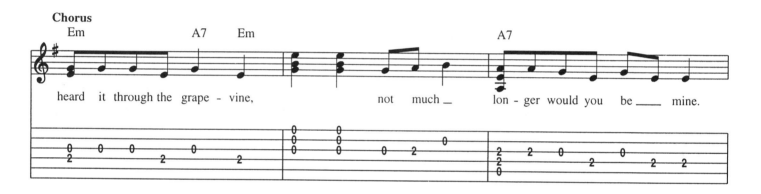

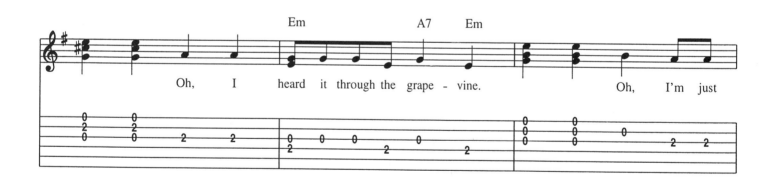

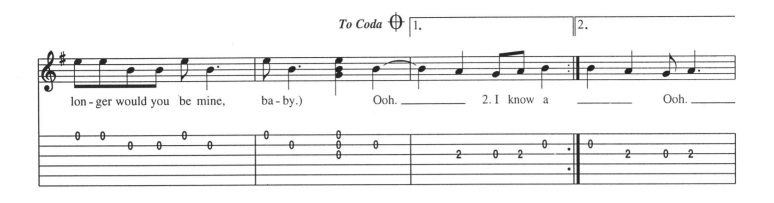

To Coda ⊕

lon-ger would you be mine, ba-by.) Ooh._____ 2. I know a _____ Ooh._____

D.S. al Coda

3. Peo-ple say be-lieve

⊕ *Coda*

Outro

Repeat & Fade

Em

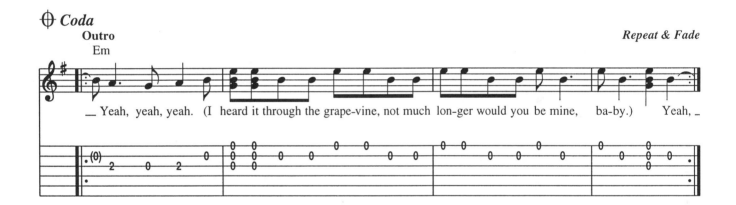

__ Yeah, yeah, yeah. (I heard it through the grape-vine, not much lon-ger would you be mine, ba-by.) Yeah, _

Additional Lyrics

2. I know a man ain't supposed to cry, but these tears I can't hold inside.
   Losin' you would end my life you see, 'cause you mean that much to me.
   You could have told me yourself that you loved someone else.

3. People say believe half of what you see, son, and none of what you hear.
   But I can't help but be confused. If it's true, please tell me dear.
   Do you plan to let me go for the other guy you loved before?

I Love Rock 'n Roll

Words and Music by Alan Merrill and Jake Hooker

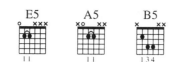

Strum Pattern: 3
Pick Pattern: 3

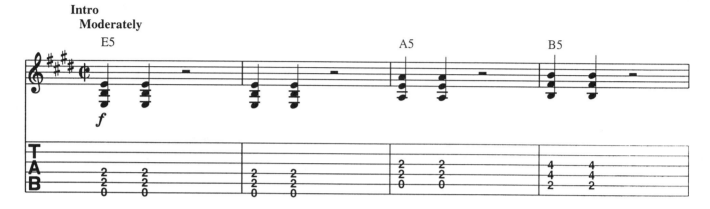

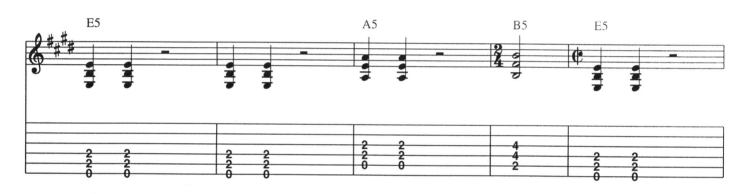

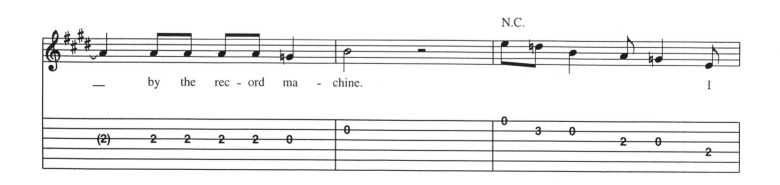

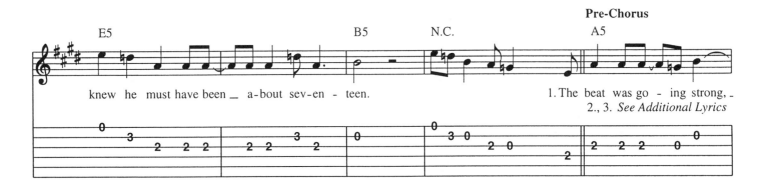

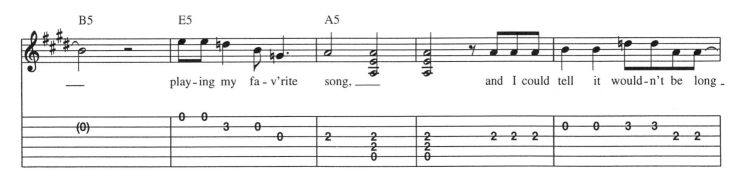

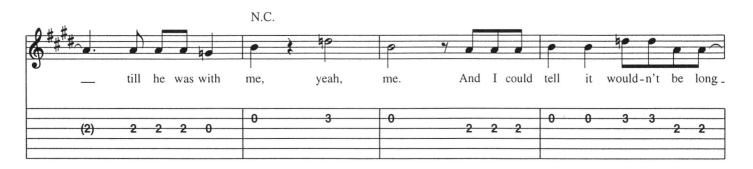

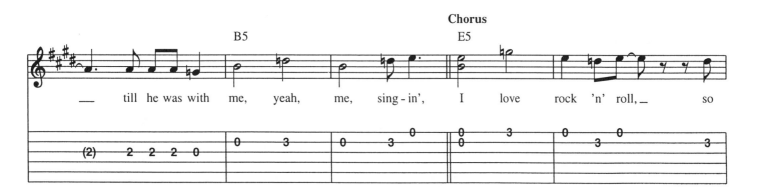

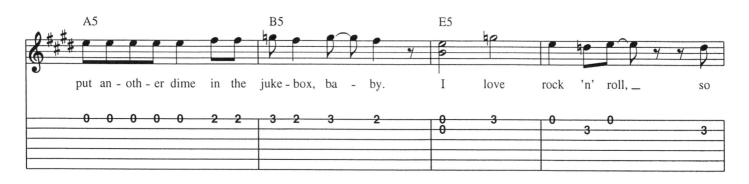

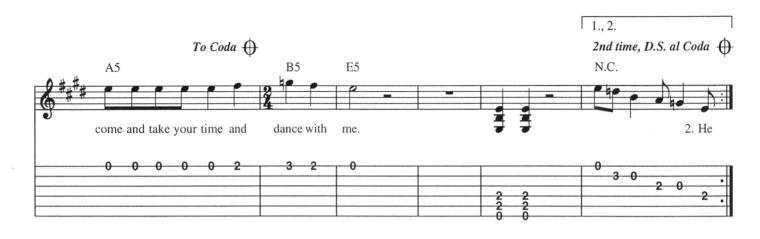

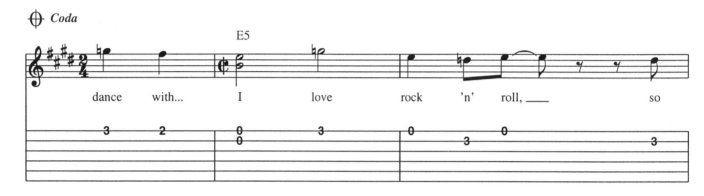

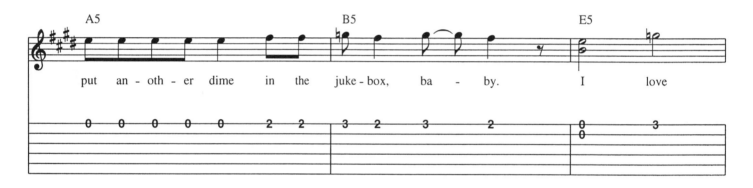

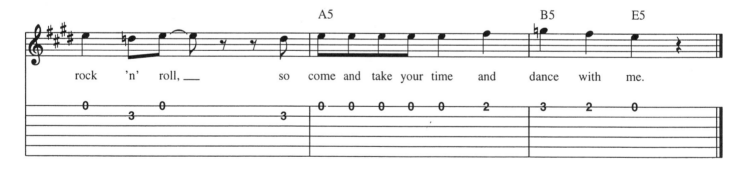

Additional Lyrics

2. He smiled, so I got up and asked for his name.
   "That don't matter," he said, "'cause it's all the same."

Pre-Chorus 2. I said, "Can I take you home where we can be alone?"
   And next, we were moving on, and he was with me, yeah, me.
   And next, we were moving on, and he was with me, yeah, me, singin',

Pre-Chorus 3. I said, "Can I take you home where we can be alone?"
   Next, we were moving on, and he was with me, yeah, me.
   And we'll be moving on and singin' that same old song, yeah, with me, singin',

I Saw Her Standing There

Words and Music by John Lennon and Paul McCartney

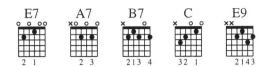

Strum Pattern: 1, 6
Pick Pattern: 2, 4

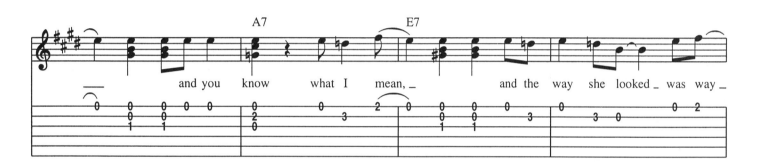

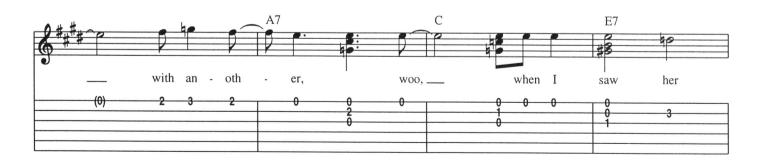

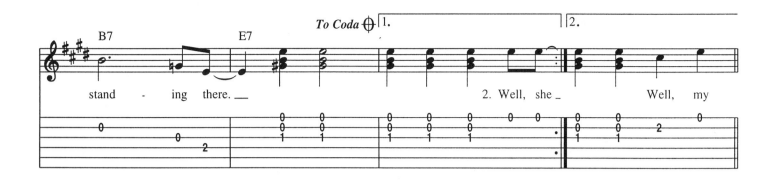

stand - ing there. __ 2. Well, she _ Well, my

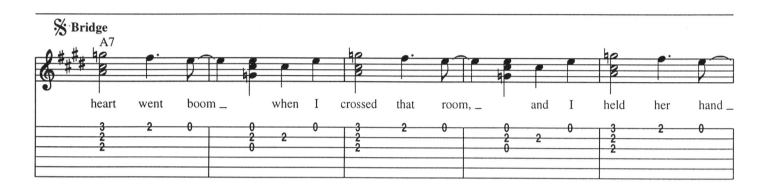

Bridge

heart went boom _ when I crossed that room, _ and I held her hand _

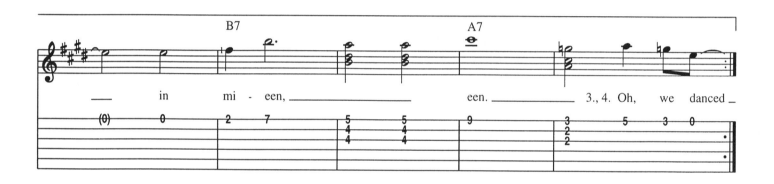

__ in mi - een, _____ een. _____ 3., 4. Oh, we danced _

3.

Guitar Solo

D.S. al Coda
(take repeat)

Coda

Outro

Well, my

Oh, since I saw __ her stand - ing there. __
Yeah, well since I saw __ her stand - ing there. __

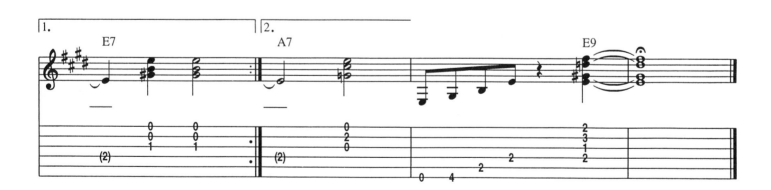

Additional Lyrics

2. Well, she looked at me
And I, I could see
That before too long
I'd fall in love with her.
She wouldn't dance with another, woo,
When I saw her standing there.

3., 4. Oh, we danced through the night
And we held each other tight,
And before too long
I fell in love with her.
Now I'll never dance with another, woo,
Since I saw her standing there.

Love Song

Words and Music by Jeff Keith and Frank Hannon

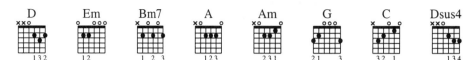

Strum Pattern: 2, 4
Pick Pattern: 2, 4

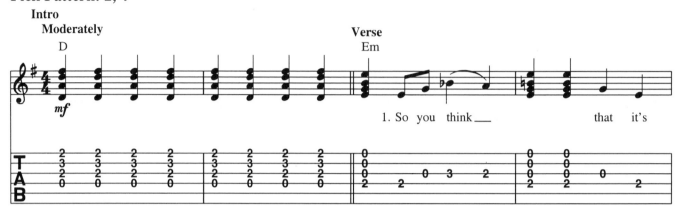

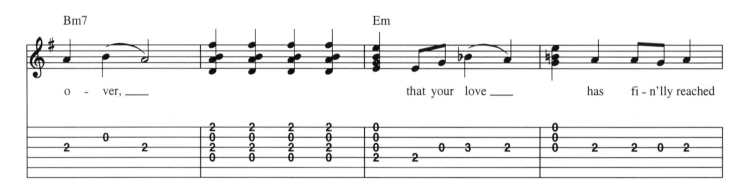

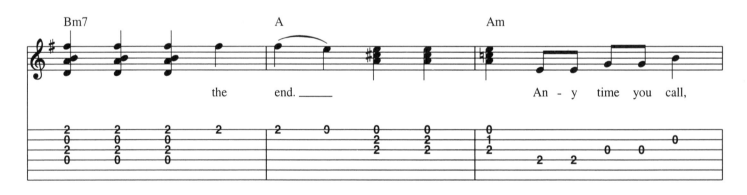

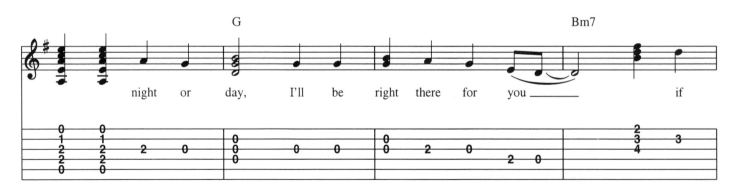

114

you need a friend. ___   It's gon - na

take a lit - tle time. ___   I know.   Time is sure

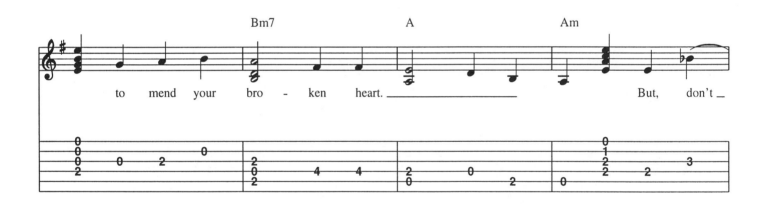

to mend your bro - ken heart. _____   But, don't _

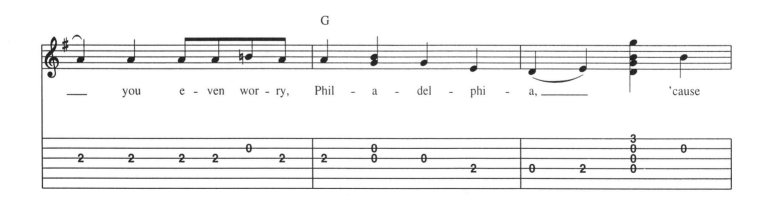

___ you e - ven wor - ry, Phil - a - del - phi - a, _____   'cause

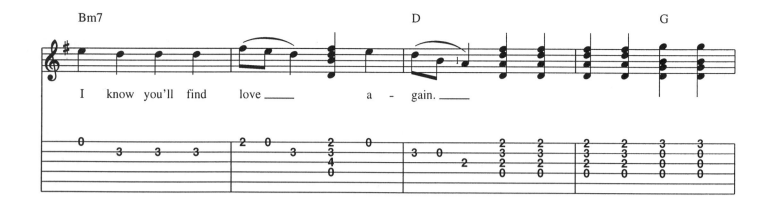

I know you'll find love ____ a - gain. ____

New York. Ooh, yeah. ____

Chorus

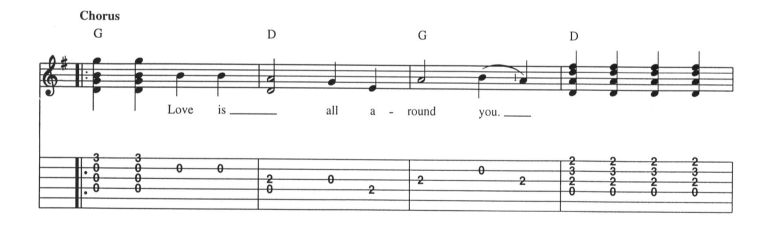

Love is ____ all a - round you. ____

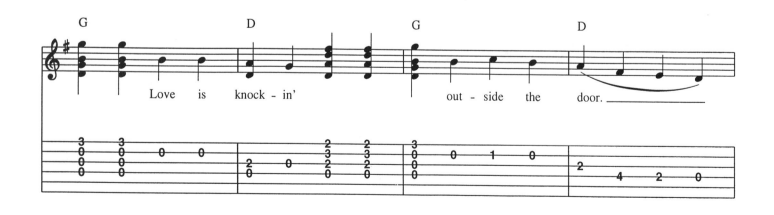

Love is knock - in' out - side the door. ____

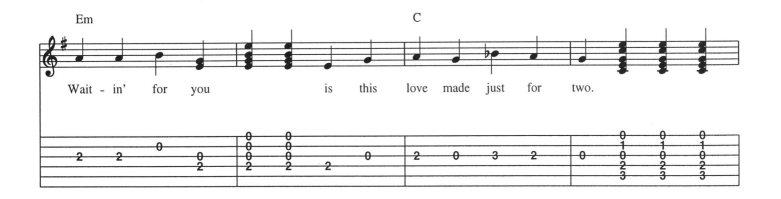

Waitin' for you is this love made just for two.

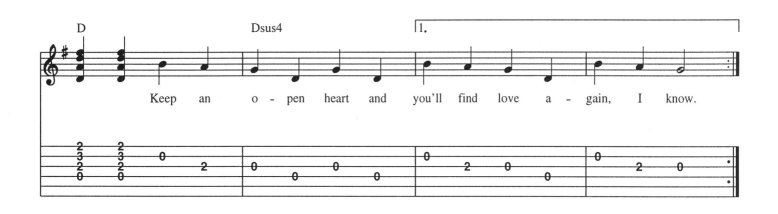

Keep an o-pen heart and you'll find love a-gain, I know.

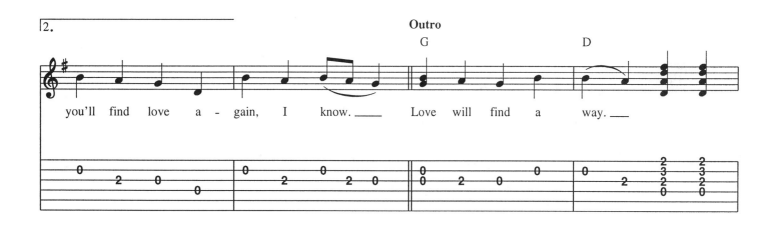

you'll find love a-gain, I know. ___ Love will find a way. ___

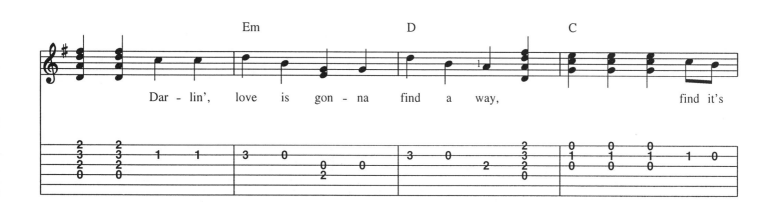

Dar-lin', love is gon-na find a way, find it's

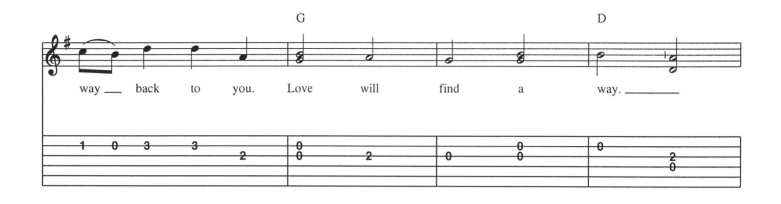

way __ back to you. Love will find a way. _____

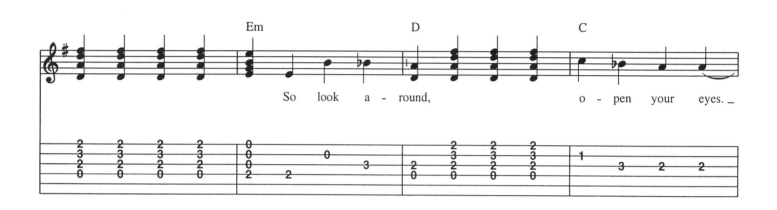

So look a - round, o - pen your eyes. _

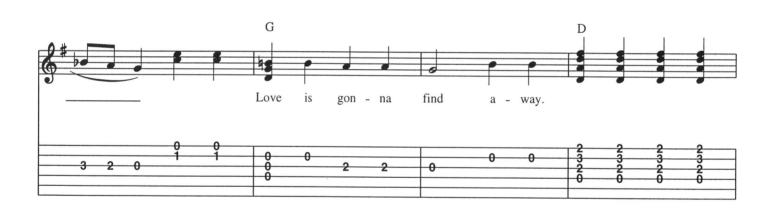

_____ Love is gon - na find a - way.

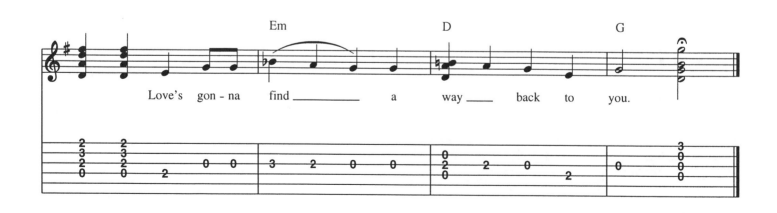

Love's gon - na find _____ a way __ back to you.

Malagueña

from the Spanish Suite ANDALUCIA

Music and Spanish Lyric by Ernesto Lecuona
English Lyric by Marian Banks

Strum Pattern: 8
Pick Pattern: 8

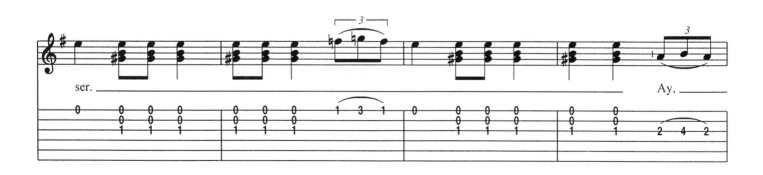

Slower

Ma - la - gue - ña de o - jos ne - gros, _____ Ma - la - gue - ña de mis

sue - ños, _____ si no me quie - res me mue - ro. _____

Freely

Ah, _____ ah, _____ ah, _____ ah. _____

Moderately

Tra - la - ra - la - ra - la, tra - la - ra - la - rá, tra - la - ra - la -

rá - la - rá - la - rá - la - rá! _____

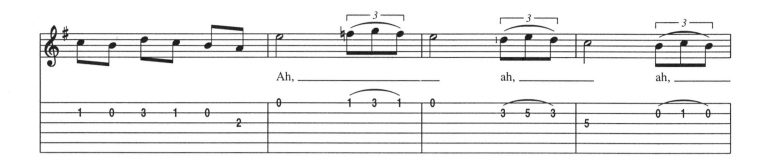

Ah, _____ ah, _____ ah,

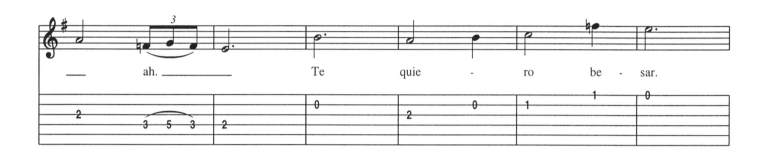

— ah. _____ Te quie - ro be - sar.

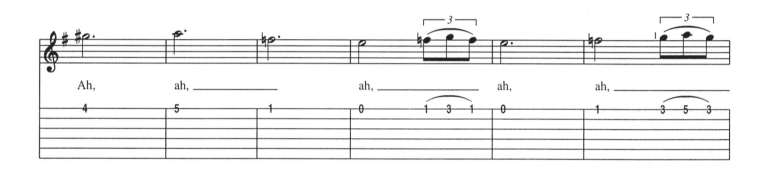

Ah, ah, _____ ah, _____ ah, ah, _____

— ah, _____

ah. _____ ¡O - lé!

Me and Bobby McGee

Words and Music by Kris Kristofferson and Fred Foster

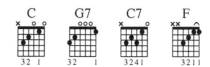

Strum Pattern: 1, 3
Pick Pattern: 1, 3

Verse
Moderately

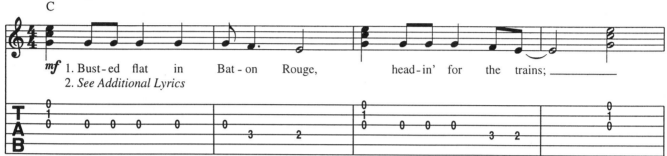

1. Bust-ed flat in Bat-on Rouge, head-in' for the trains;
2. *See Additional Lyrics*

feel-in' near-ly fad-ed as my jeans.

Bob-by thumbed a die-sel down just be-fore it rained;

took us all the way to New Or - leans.

Feel-in' good was eas - y, Lord, _ when _____ Bob-by sang the blues. _____

{ Feel - in' good was good e - nough _ for me, _____
{ And bud - dy, that was good e - nough _ for me, _____

good e - nough for me and Bob - by Mc - Gee. _

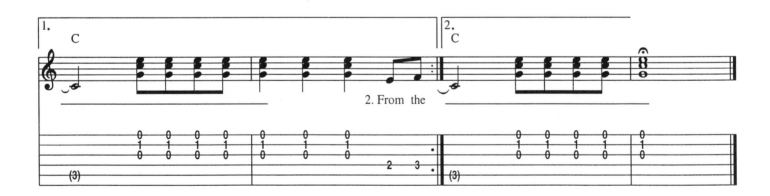

2. From the

Additional Lyrics

2. From the coal mines of Kentucky to the California sun,
   Bobby shared the secrets of my soul.
   Standin' right beside me, Lord, through ev'rything I dare,
   And ev'ry night she kept me from the cold.
   Then somewhere near Salinas, Lord, I let her slip away.
   Lookin' for the home I hope she'll find.
   And I'd trade all of my tomorrows for a single yesterday,
   Holdin' Bobby's body next to mine.

Runaway

Words and Music by Del Shannon and Max Crook

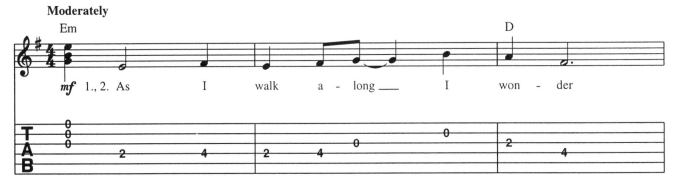

Strum Pattern: 6
Pick Pattern: 4

Verse
Moderately

1., 2. As I walk a - long ___ I won - der

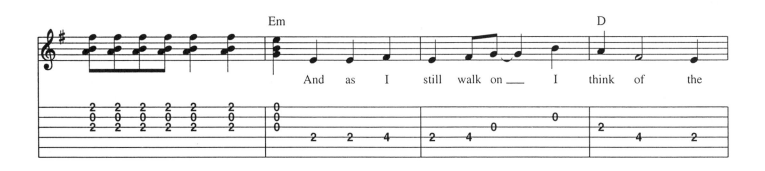

what went wrong ___ with our love, a love that was ___ so strong.

And as I still walk on ___ I think of the

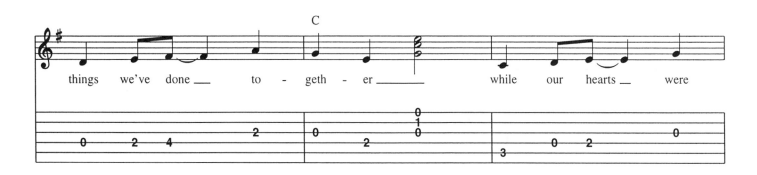

things we've done ___ to - geth - er ___ while our hearts ___ were

young. I'm a-walk-in'

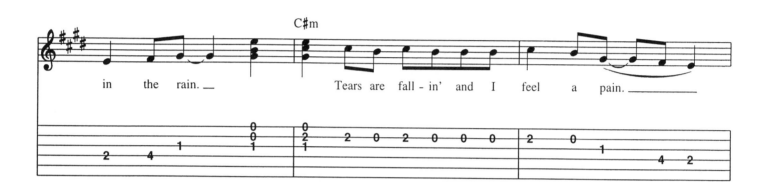

in the rain. ___ Tears are fall-in' and I feel a pain. ___

A-wish-in' you were here by me ___ to end this

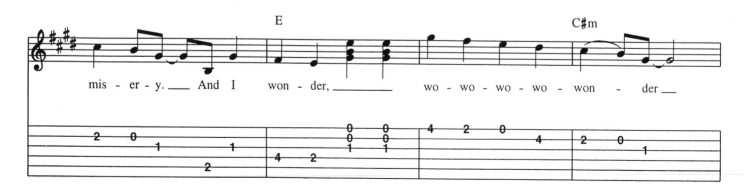

mis-er-y. ___ And I won-der, ___ wo-wo-wo-wo-won-der ___

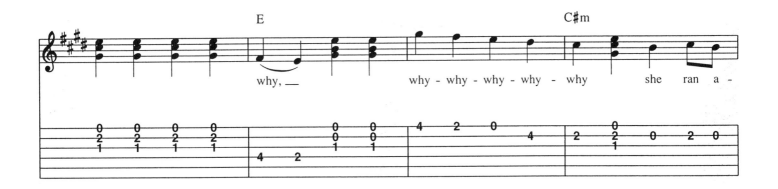

why, ___ why - why - why - why - why she ran a -

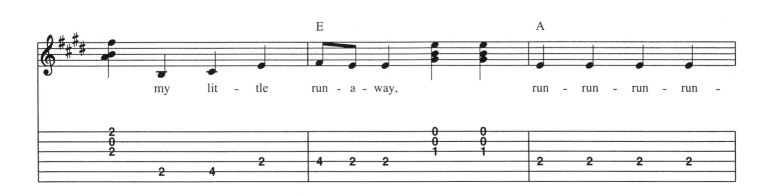

way. And I ___ won - der ___ where she will stay, ___

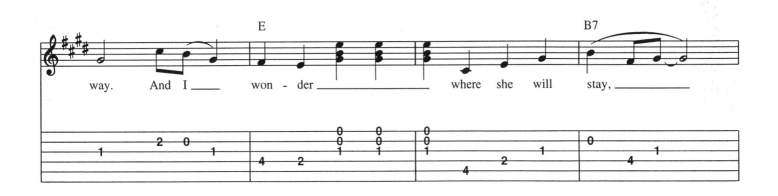

my lit - tle run - a - way, run - run - run - run -

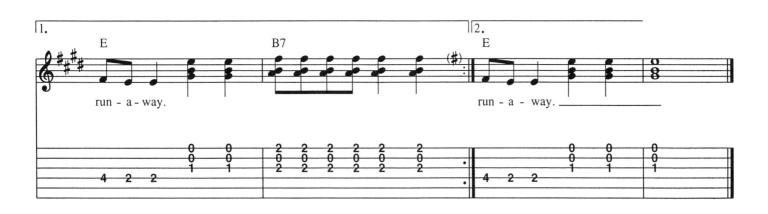

run - a - way. run - a - way. ___

Oklahoma
from OKLAHOMA!

Lyrics by Oscar Hammerstein II
Music by Richard Rodgers

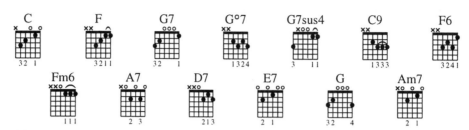

Strum Pattern: 10
Pick Pattern: 10

Intro
Lively

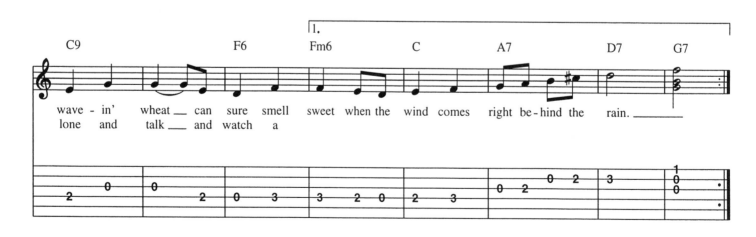

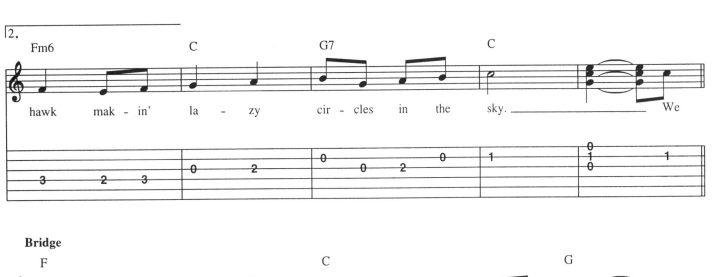

Bridge

Outro

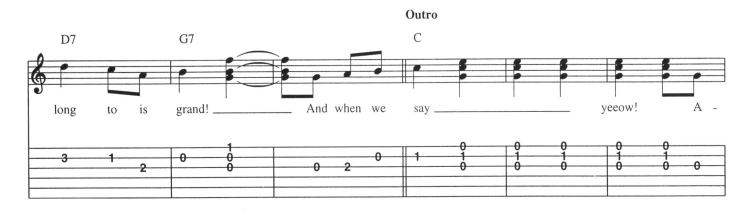

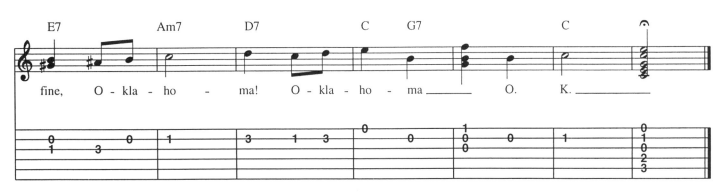

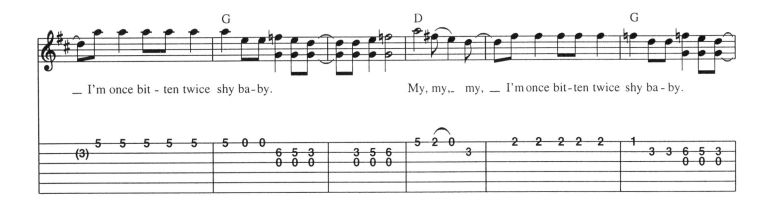

I'm once bit-ten twice shy ba-by. My, my,_ my, _ I'm once bit-ten twice shy ba-by.

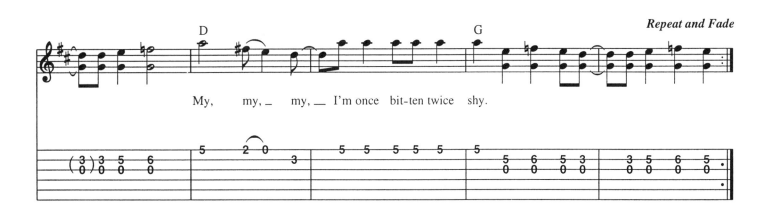

Repeat and Fade

My, my,_ my, _ I'm once bit-ten twice shy.

Additional Lyrics

2. Now it's the middle of the night on the open road.
The heater don't work and it's oh so cold.
You're lookin' tired, you're lookin' kind-a beat.
The rhythm of the street sure knocks you off your feet.

Pre-Chorus 2. You didn't know how rock and roll looked
Until you caught your sister with the guys from the group.
Halfway home in the parking lot,
By the look in her eye she was givin' what she got.
I said …

3. Oh, woman you're a mess, gonna die in your sleep.
There's blood on my amp and my Les Paul's beat.
Can't keep you home, you're messin' around.
My best friend told me you're the best lick in town.

Pre-Chorus 3. You didn't know that rock and roll burned
So you bought a candle and you lived and learned.
You got the rhythm. You got the speed.
Ma-ma's little baby likes it short and sweet.
I said…

Pre-Chorus 4. I didn't know you had a rock and roll record
Until I saw your picture on another guy's jacket.
You told me I was the only one.
But look at you now, it's as dark as it's gone.
I said…

To Coda 1 ✛   *To Coda 2* ✛   **Verse**

high a-bove __ me. ____   2. First class and fan-

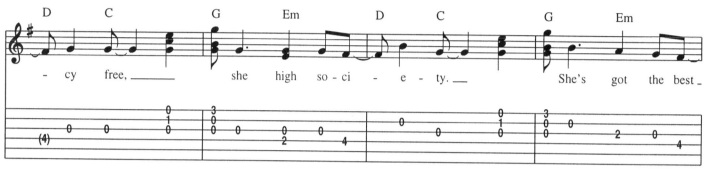

-cy free, _____ she high so-ci-e-ty. __   She's got the best __

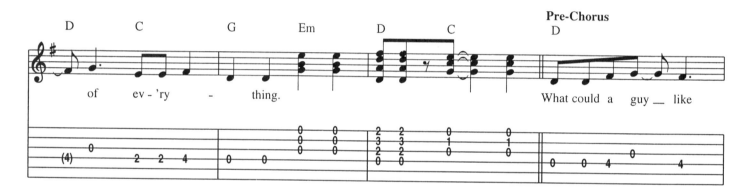

Pre-Chorus

of ev-'ry - thing.   What could a guy __ like

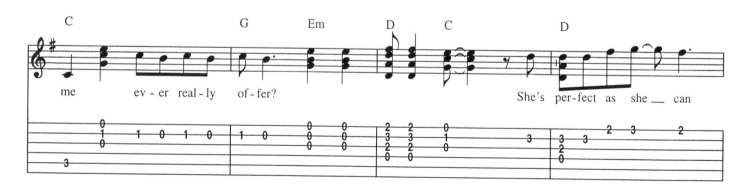

me ev-er real-ly of-fer?   She's per-fect as she __ can

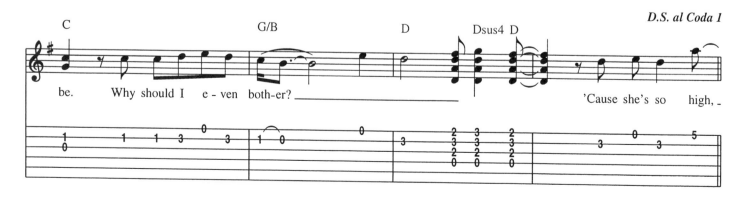

D.S. al Coda 1

be. Why should I e-ven both-er? _____ 'Cause she's so high, __

D.S.S. al Coda 2

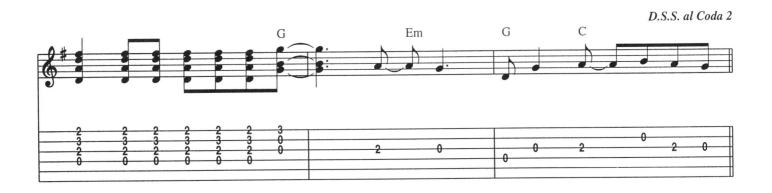

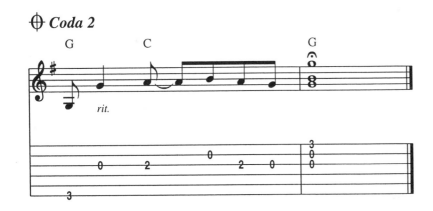

Additional Lyrics

3. She calls to speak to me.
   I freeze immediately.
   'Cause what she says sounds so unreal.

Stand By Me

Words and Music by Ben E. King, Jerry Leiber and Mike Stoller

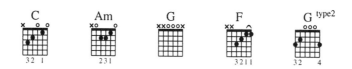

Strum Pattern: 2
Pick Pattern: 4

Verse

Moderately

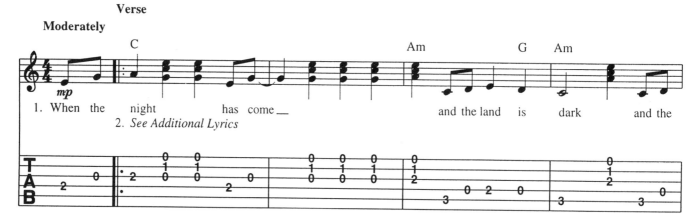

1. When the night has come __ and the land is dark and the
2. *See Additional Lyrics*

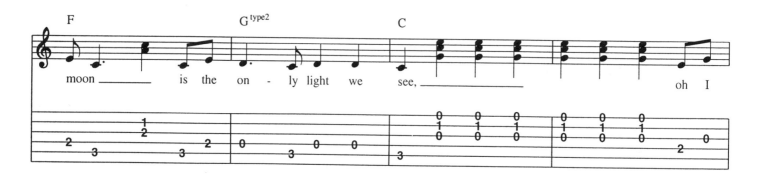

moon __ is the on-ly light we see, __ oh I

won't be a-fraid, __ no I __ won't be a-fraid __ just as

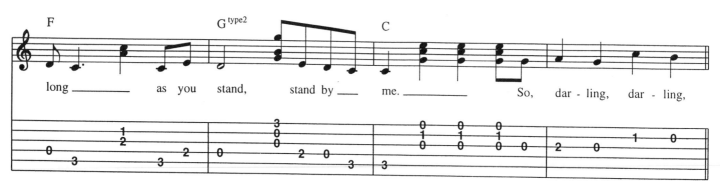

long __ as you stand, stand by __ me. __ So, dar-ling, dar-ling,

Additional Lyrics

2. If the sky that we look upon should tumble and fall
   And the mountains should crumble into the sea,
   I won't cry, I won't cry, no I won't shed a tear
   Just as long as you stand, stand by me.

Tears in Heaven

Words and Music by Eric Clapton and Will Jennings

'cause I know I don't be - long _____ here in heav -

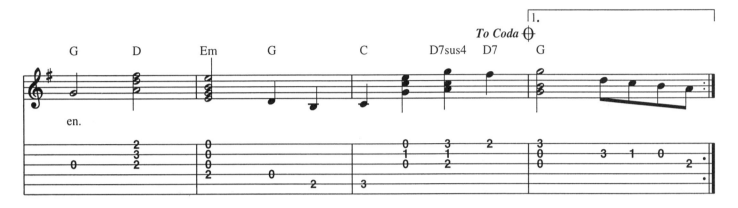

en.

To Coda ⊕

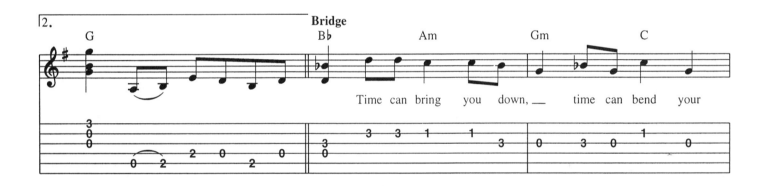

Bridge

Time can bring you down, __ time can bend your

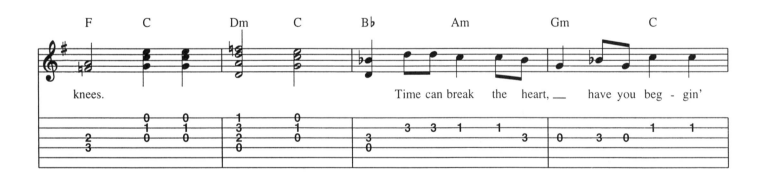

knees.　　　　　　　　　Time can break the heart, __ have you beg - gin'

Guitar Solo

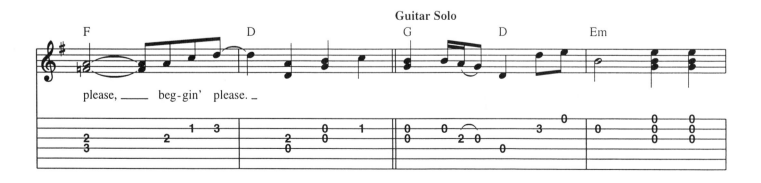

please, ___ beg-gin' please. _

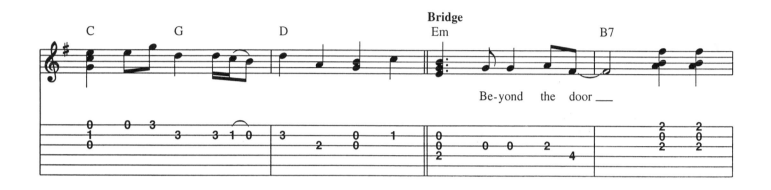

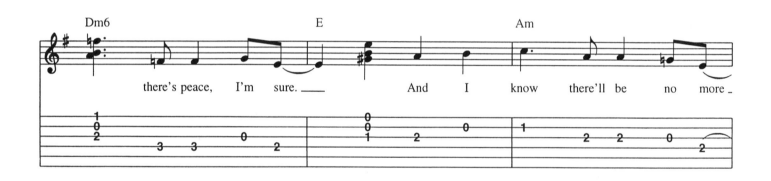

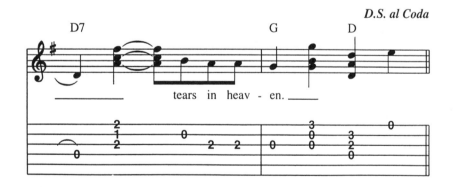

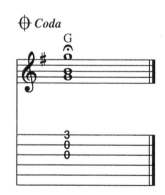

Additional Lyrics

2. Would you hold my hand
   If I saw you in heaven?
   Would you help me stand
   If I saw you in heaven?
   I'll find my way through night and day,
   'Cause I know I just can't stay here in heaven.

That'll Be the Day

Words and Music by Jerry Allison, Norman Petty and Buddy Holly

Strum Pattern: 1
Pick Pattern: 2

Intro
Moderately

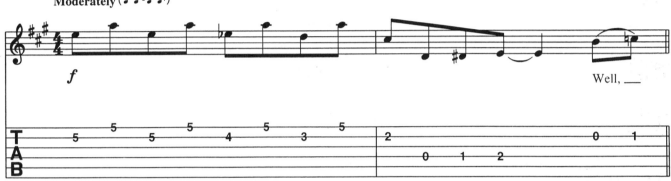

Well, ___

Chorus

that-'ll be the day, when you say good-bye. Yes, that-'ll be the day, when

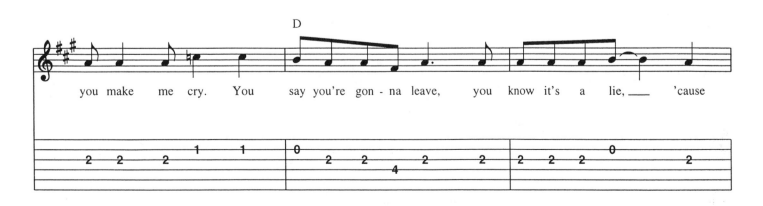

you make me cry. You say you're gon-na leave, you know it's a lie, ___ 'cause

To Coda ⊕

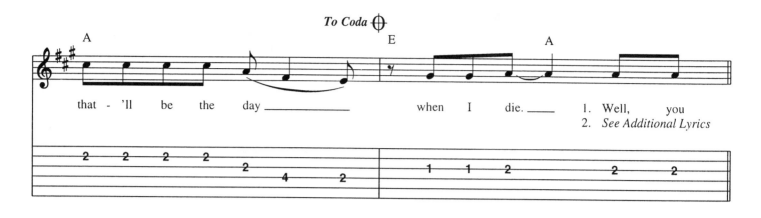

that - 'll be the day _____ when I die. ____ 1. Well, you
2. *See Additional Lyrics*

Verse

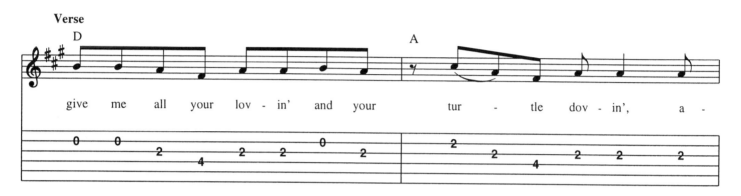

give me all your lov - in' and your tur - tle dov - in', a -

all your hugs and kiss - es and your mon - ey too. ____ Well, ___ a -

you know you love me ba - by, still ____ you tell me, may - be,

2nd time, D.S. al Coda

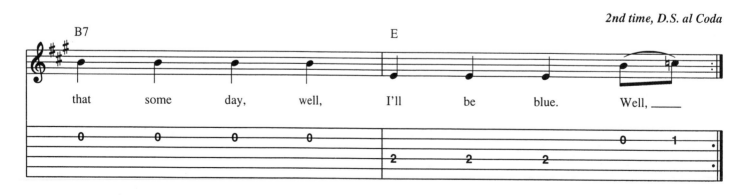

that some day, well, I'll be blue. Well, _____

when I die. ___ Well, ___ that - 'll be the day, ooh. ___

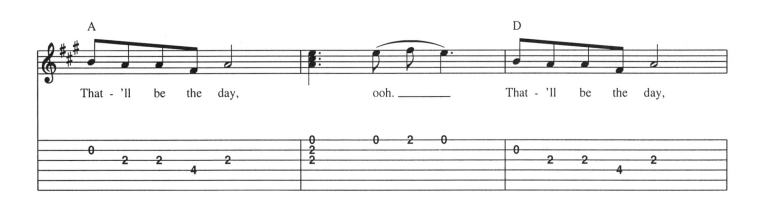

That - 'll be the day, ooh. ___ That - 'll be the day,

ooh. ___ That - 'll be the day.

Additional Lyrics

2. Well, when cupid shot his dart,
   He shot it at your heart,
   So if we ever part then I'll leave you.
   You sit and hold me and you
   Tell me boldly, that some day,
   Well, I'll be through.

To Be With You

Words and Music by Eric Martin and David Grahame

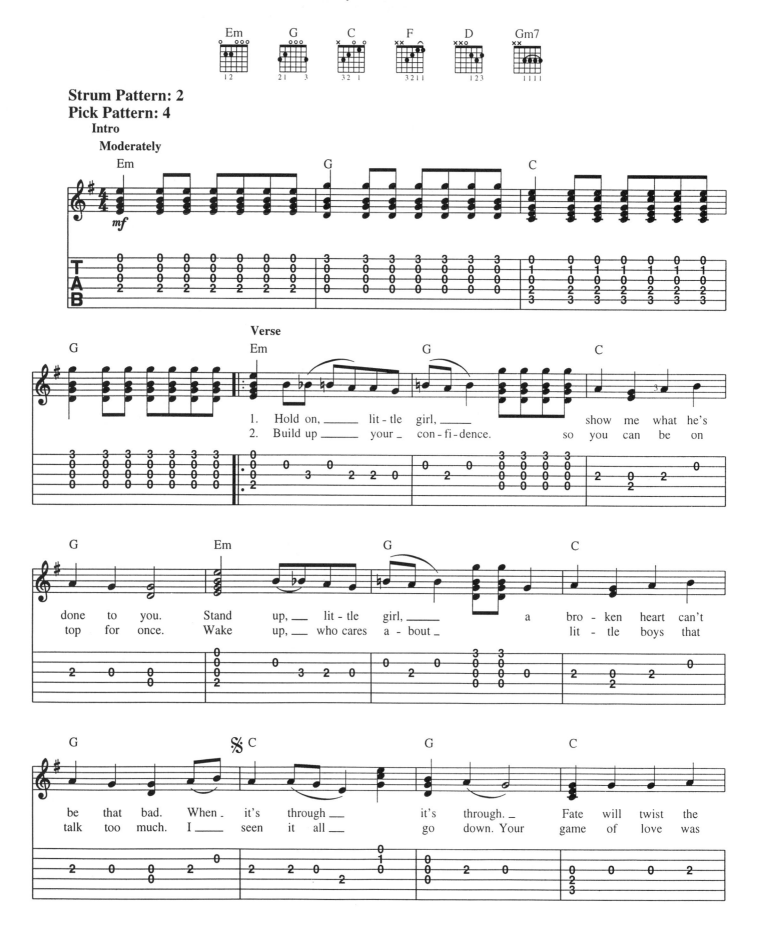

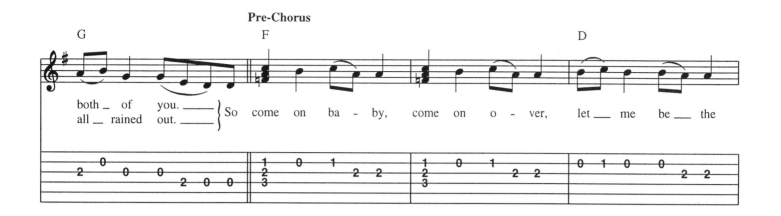

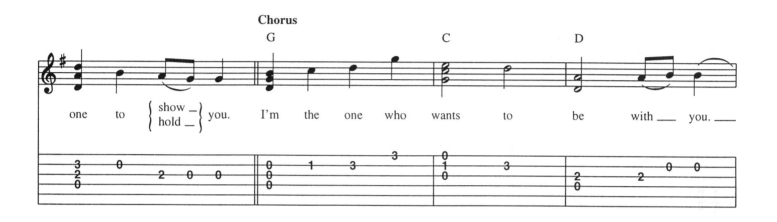

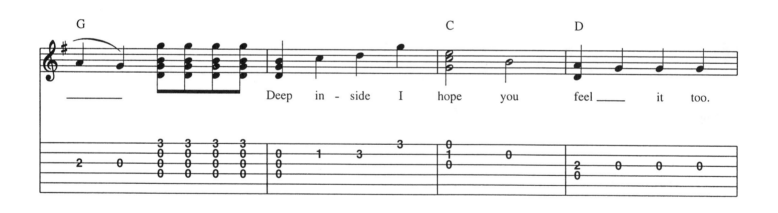

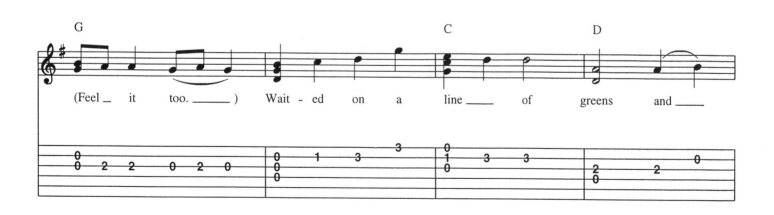

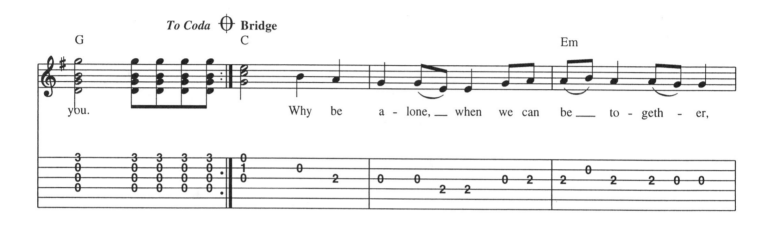

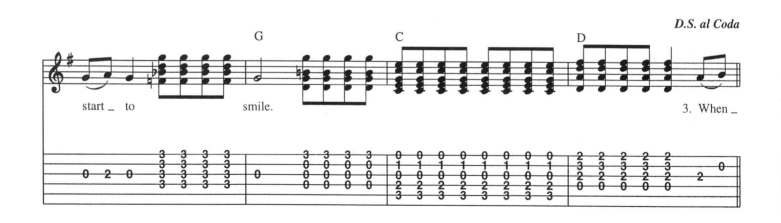

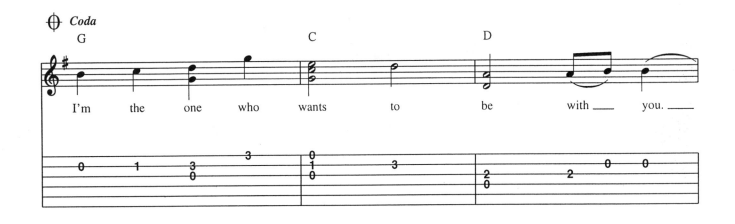

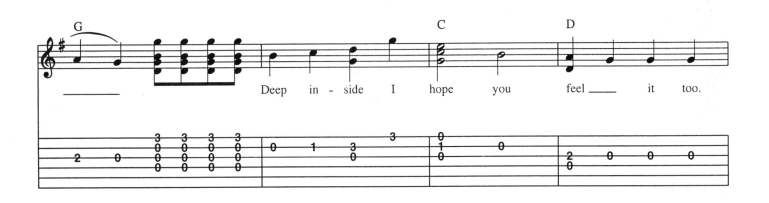

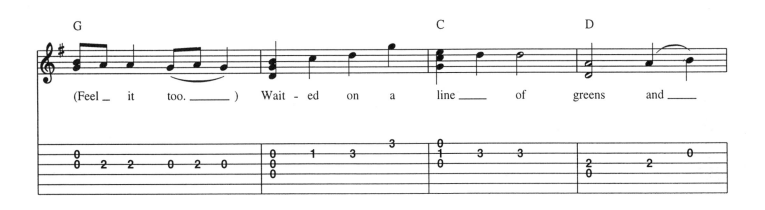

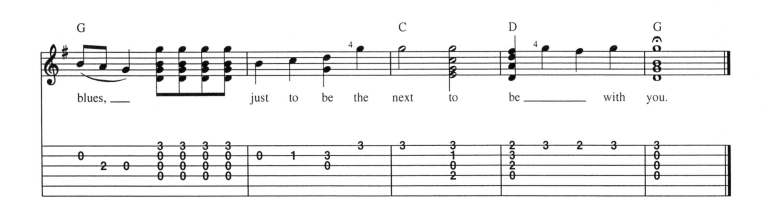

Turn! Turn! Turn!
(To Everything There Is a Season)

Words from the Book of Ecclesiastes
Adaptation and Music by Pete Seeger

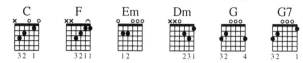

Strum Pattern: 4, 5
Pick Pattern: 4, 5

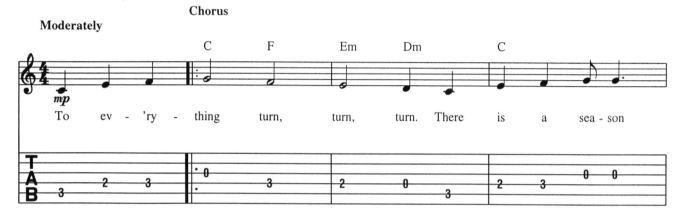

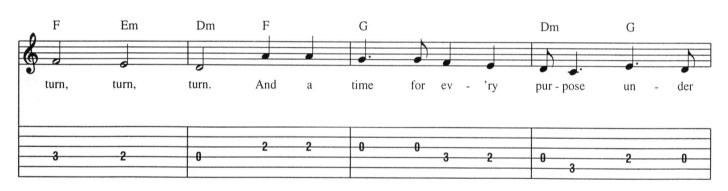

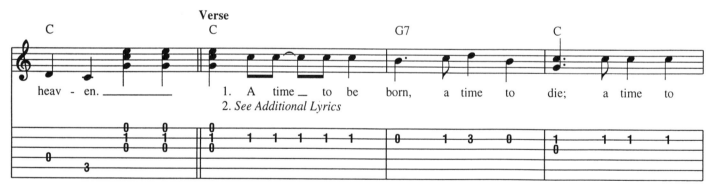

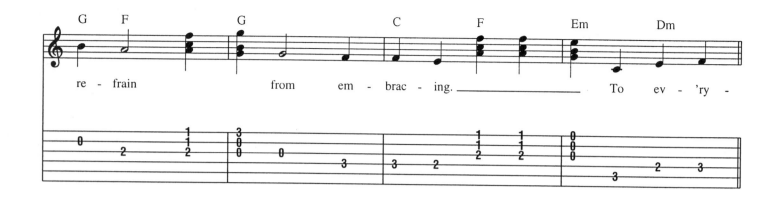

re - frain   from   em - brac - ing. _____   To   ev - 'ry -

Chorus

thing   turn,   turn,   turn. There   is   a   sea - son   turn,   turn,   turn.   And   a

time   for   ev - 'ry   pur - pose   un - der   heav - en. _____   heav - en. ____

Additional Lyrics

2. A time to build up, a time to break down;
   A time to dance, a time to mourn;
   A time to cast away stones,
   A time to gather stones together.

4. A time to gain, a time to lose;
   A time to bend, a time to sew;
   A time to love, a time to hate;
   A time for peace, I swear it's not too late.

You Got It

Words and Music by Roy Orbison, Jeff Lynne and Tom Petty

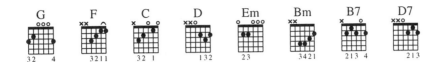

Strum Pattern: 4
Pick Pattern: 5

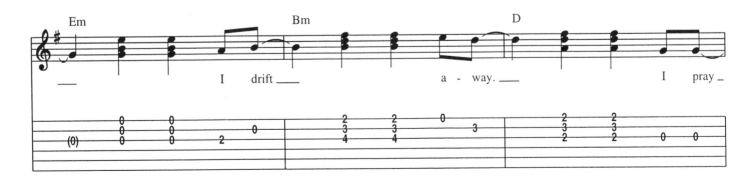

156

Additional Lyrics

2. Every time I hold you I begin to understand.
   Everything about you tells me I'm your man.

Pre-Chorus 2. I live my life to be with you.
   No one can do the things you do.

Pre-Chorus 3. I'm glad to give my love to you.
   I know you feel the way I do.

Your Cheatin' Heart

Words and Music by Hank Williams

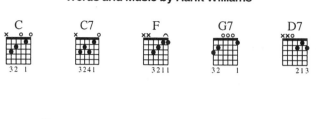

Strum Pattern: 3
Pick Pattern: 3

Verse

Moderately Fast

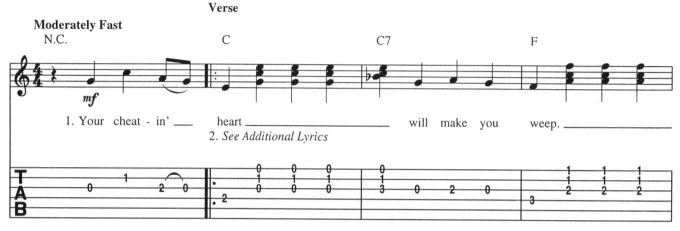

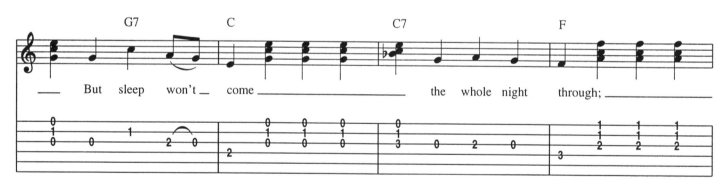

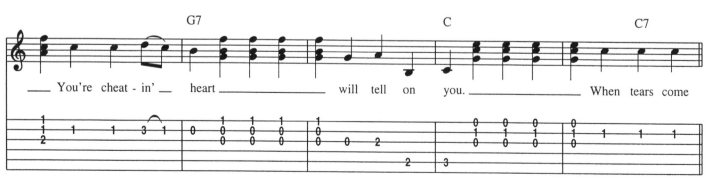

Bridge

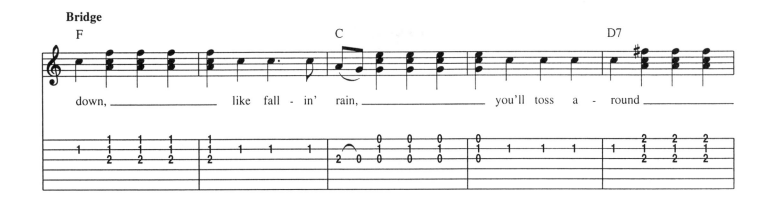

down, _____ like fall - in' rain, _____ you'll toss a - round _____

Outro

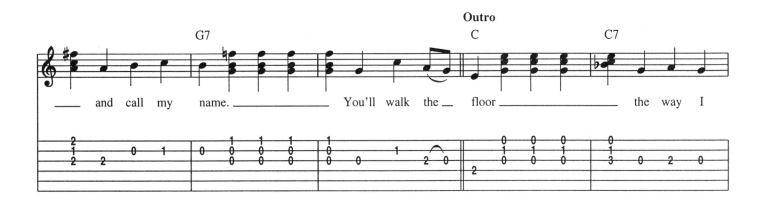

___ and call my name. _____ You'll walk the _ floor _____ the way I

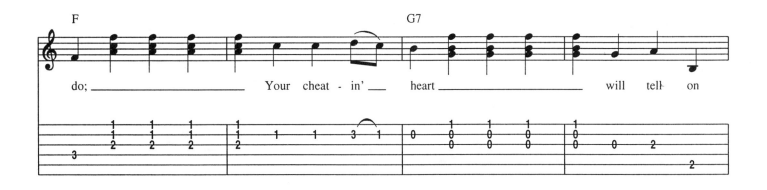

do; _____ Your cheat - in' ___ heart _____ will tell on

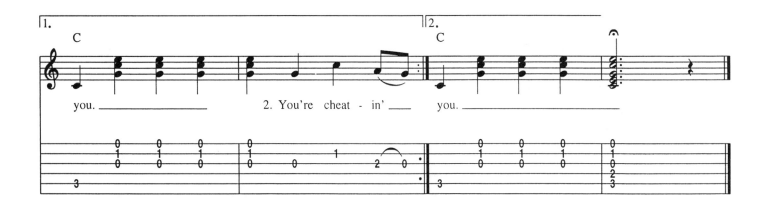

you. _____ 2. You're cheat - in' ___ you. _____

Additional Lyrics

2. Your cheatin' heart will pine someday,
And crave the love you threw away.
The time will come when you'll be blue;
Your cheatin' heart will tell on you.

Baby Love

Words and Music by Brian Holland, Edward Holland and Lamont Dozier

Strum Pattern: 3
Pick Pattern: 3

Verse

Moderately

1. Ba - by love, my ba - by love, I need you, oh, how I need _ you.
2., 3. *See Additional Lyrics*

But all you do is treat me bad, _____ break my heart and leave me sad. _____

Wan-na know what did I do wrong _ to make you stay a - way so long. 'Cause ba-by love, my

ba-by love, been miss-ing ya, miss _ kiss-ing ya. In - stead of break-ing up, _____

let's start some kiss-ing and mak-ing up. _____ Don't throw our love a - way. _____

1. In my arms why don't you stay?

2. got the best of

D.C. al Coda

Coda

hurt me, till it

hurt me. Ooh, _____ ba - by love,

Outro / *Repeat and Fade*

don't throw our love a - way.

Additional Lyrics

2. Baby love, my baby love, why must we separate my love?
All of my whole life through, I never love no one but you.
Why you do me like you do, I guess it's me, ooh.
Need to hold you once again my love, feel your warm embrace my love.
Don't throw our love away, please don't do me this way.
Not happy like I used to be. Loneliness has got the best of

3. Me my love, my baby love, I need ya, oh, how I need ya.
Why you do me like you do, after I've been true to you.
So deep in love with you. Baby, baby, ooh.
Till it hurt me, till it hurt me.
Ooh, baby love, don't throw our love a-way.

Chariots of Fire

Music by Vangelis

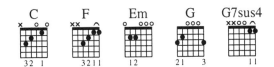

Strum Pattern: 4
Pick Pattern: 1

Cheek to Cheek

from the RKO Radio Motion Picture TOP HAT

Words and Music by Irving Berlin

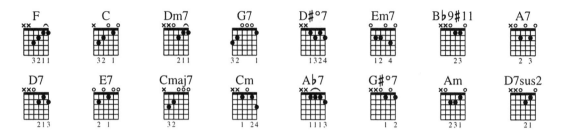

Strum Pattern: 4
Pick Pattern: 5

Chorus
Moderately

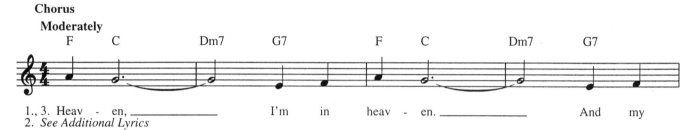

1., 3. Heav - en, _____ I'm in heav - en. _____ And my
2. *See Additional Lyrics*

heart beats so that I can hard - ly speak. _____ And I

seem to find the hap - pi - ness I seek. _____ when we're

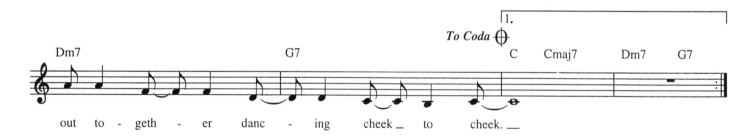

out to - geth - er danc - ing cheek _ to cheek. _

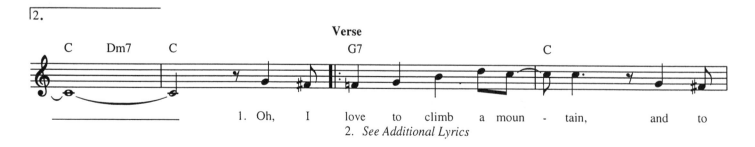

1. Oh, I love to climb a moun - tain, and to
2. *See Additional Lyrics*

reach the high-est peak. __ But it does-n't thrill me half as much __ as

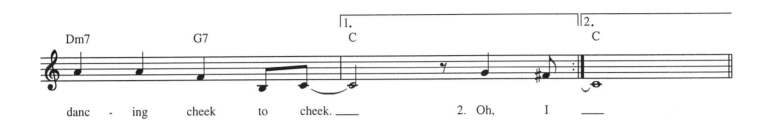

danc - ing cheek to cheek. ____ 2. Oh, I __

Bridge

Dance with me. _____ I want my arm a - bout you. _____ The

D.C. al Coda

charm a - bout you _____ will car - ry me thru _____ to. . .

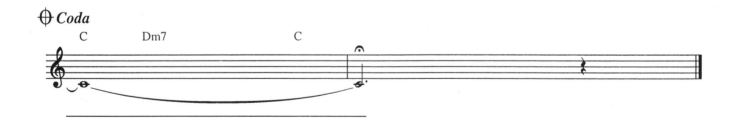

⊕ *Coda*

Additional Lyrics

Chorus   2. Heaven, I'm in heaven.
And the cares that hung around me thru the week
Seem to vanish like a gambler's lucky streak
When we're out together dancing cheek to cheek.

2. Oh, I love to go out fishing
In a river or a creek.
But I don't enjoy it half as much
As dancing cheek to cheek.

Drive My Car

Words and Music by John Lennon and Paul McCartney

Strum Pattern: 3
Pick Pattern: 4

Additional Lyrics

2. I told that girl that my prospects were good.
   She said, "Baby, it's understood,
   Working for peanuts is all very fine,
   But I can show you a better time.

3. I told that girl I could start right away,
   She said, "Baby, I've got something to say.
   I got no car and it's breakin' my heart,
   But I've found a driver, that's a start.

Emotions

Lyrics by Mariah Carey

Music by Mariah Carey, David Cole and Robert Clivilles

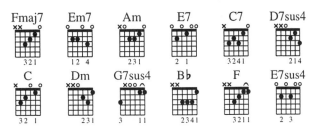

Strum Pattern: 2
Pick Pattern: 4

Intro
Moderate Dance Tempo

Chorus

You've got me feel-ing e - mo - tions ___ deep - er than I've ev - er dreamed of. ___

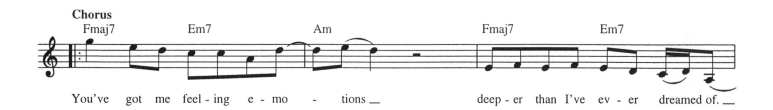

___ Whoa, _ oh. ___ You've got me feel - ing ___ e - mo - tions ___

Verse

high - er than the heav - ens a - bove. ___ 1. I feel good, _ I feel nice. _

2. *See Additional Lyrics*

I've nev-er felt __ so __ sat-is-fied. __ I'm in love, __ I'm a-live. __

Pre-Chorus

In-tox-i-cat-ed, fly-ing high. _____ It feels like a dream __

_____ when you {touch __ / love __} me ten - der - ly. _____

1.

{ I don't know __ if it's real _____ / I don't know if you're __ for real _____ } but I like the way I feel _____ in - side.

2.   **Chorus**

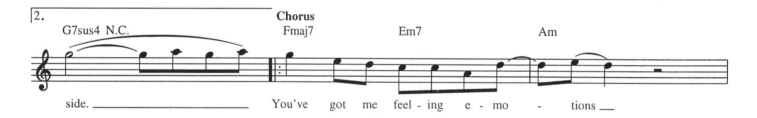

side. _____ You've got me feel-ing e - mo - tions __

deep-er than I've ev-er dreamed of. _____ Whoa, __ oh. ____ You've got me feel-ing ____ e -

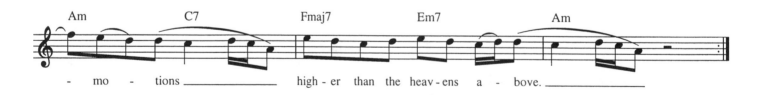

- mo - tions _____ high-er than the heav-ens a - bove. _____

Bridge

You know __ the __ way __ to make __ me lose __ con - trol. _____

166

B♭ ... **F** ... **E7sus4**

When you're look-ing in-to ___ my ___ eyes ___ you make me feel so ___

Interlude

E7 ... **Fmaj7** **N.C.**

high! ___

Am ... **E7** ... **Dm** **Em7** ... **G7sus4 N.C.**

Outro-Chorus

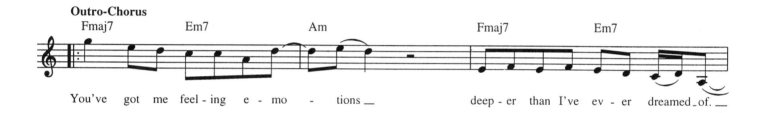

Fmaj7 ... **Em7** ... **Am** ... **Fmaj7** ... **Em7**

You've got me feel-ing e - mo - tions ___ deep-er than I've ev-er dreamed of. ___

Am ... **Fmaj7** ... **E7** ... **Am** ... **C7**

Whoa, ___ oh. ___ You've got me feel-ing ___ e - mo - tions ___

Fmaj7 ... **Em7** ... 1. **Am** ... 2. **Am** ... **N.C.**

high-er than the heav-ens a - bove. ___ ___ You've got me feel-ing high - er.

Additional Lyrics

2. In the morning when I rise
   You are the first thing on my mind.
   And in the middle of the night
   I feel your heart next to mine.

Emotional Rescue

Words and Music by Mick Jagger and Keith Richards

Help Me

By Sonny Boy Williamson, Ralph Bass and Willie Dixon

Strum Pattern: 3
Pick Pattern: 4

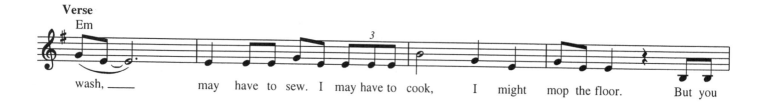

help me, dar - ling, __ I'll find my - self some-bod - y else. 3. When I

Verse

walk, _____ you walk with me. And when I talk, you talk to me. Oh,

babe, I can't do it all by my - self. If you don't

help me dar - ling, __ I'll have to find some-bod - y else. 4. Bring my night -

Verse

shirt. Put on your morn - ing gown. _____ Oh,

bring me my night-shirt. Put on your morn - ing gown. Do not know

where she been but I feel like ly - in' down.

In the Mood

By Joe Garland

Strum Pattern: 1, 3
Pick Pattern: 2, 3

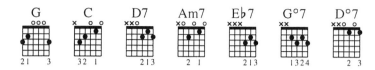

last time, Fine

C

D.S al Fine
(take repeat)

D

Lay Down Sally

Words and Music by Eric Clapton, Marcy Levy and George Terry

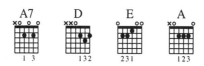

Strum Pattern: 1
Pick Pattern: 2

Intro

Bright Boogie

Verse

1. There is noth - ing that
2., 3. *See Additional Lyrics*

— is wrong — in want - ing you — to stay — here — with

me. I know you've got — some - where —

— to go, — but won't you make — your - self — at home — and

stay with me? — And don't you ev - er leave. —

%. Chorus

Lay down, Sal - ly, and rest here in __ my arms. __

Don't you think __ you want __ some - one __ to talk __ to?

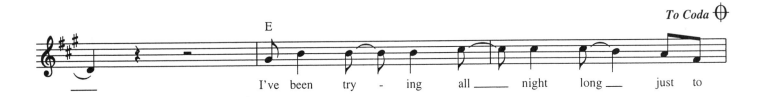

Lay down, Sal - ly. No need to leave __ so soon. __

To Coda ⊕

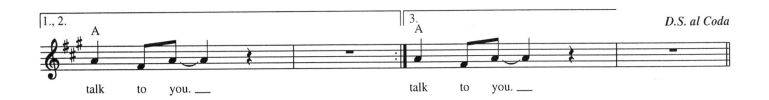

__ I've been try - ing all ____ night long __ just to

D.S. al Coda

1., 2. talk to you. __ 3. talk to you. __

⊕ *Coda*

Outro

Repeat and Fade

talk to you. __

Additional Lyrics

2. The sun ain't nearly on the rise,
   And we still got the moon and stars above.
   Underneath the velvet skies, love is all that matters.
   Won't you stay with me?
   And don't you ever leave.

3. I long to see the morning light
   Coloring your face so dreamily.
   So don't you go and say goodbye,
   You can lay your worries down and stay with me.
   And don't you ever leave.

London Bridge

Traditional

Strum Pattern: 5
Pick Pattern: 1

Chorus
Moderately

Lon - don Bridge is fall - ing down, fall - ing down, fall - ing down. Lon - don Bridge is

fall - ing down, my fair la - dy. Build it up with i - ron bars,

Verse

i - ron bars, i - ron bars. Build it up with i - ron bars, my fair la - dy.

Michael Row the Boat Ashore

Traditional Folksong

Strum Pattern: 3
Pick Pattern: 3

Slowly

Chorus

Mi - chael, row the boat a - shore, hal - le - lu - jah. Mi - chael, row the boat a -

Verse

shore, hal - le - lu - jah. 1. Sis - ter, help to trim the sail, hal - le - lu -
2., 3. *See Additional Lyrics*

jah. Sis - ter, help to trim the sail, hal - le - lu - jah! Mi - chael, jah!

1., 2.   *3.*

Additional Lyrics

2. Jordan River is chilly and cold, hal-le-lu-jah.
   Kills the body but not the soul, hal-le-lu-jah.

3. Jordan River is deep and wide, hal-le-lu-jah.
   Milk and honey on the other side, hal-le-luljah.

My Babe

Written by Willie Dixon

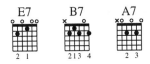

Strum Pattern: 3
Pick Pattern: 3

Verse
Moderate Blues

1. My ba - by don't stand no cheat - in', my babe.
2., 3., 4. *See Additional Lyrics*

My ba - by don't stand no cheat - in', my babe.

My ba - by don't stand no cheat-in', she don't stand none of that mid - night creep - in'.

My babe, true lit - tle ba - by, __ my babe.

Additional Lyrics

2. My babe, I know she love me, my babe.
My babe, I know she love me, my babe.
Oh yeah, I know she love me.
She don't do nothing but kiss and hug me.
My babe, true little baby, my babe.

3. My babe, she don't stand no cheatin', my babe.
My babe, she don't stand no cheatin', my babe.
Oh no, she don't stand no cheatin'.
Ev'rything she do she do so pleasin'.
My babe, true little baby, my babe.

4. My baby don't stand no fooling, my babe.
My baby don't stand no fooling, my babe.
My baby don't stand no foolin'.
When she's hot there ain't no coolin'.
My babe, true little baby, my babe.

My Funny Valentine

from BABES IN ARMS
Words by Lorenz Hart
Music by Richard Rodgers

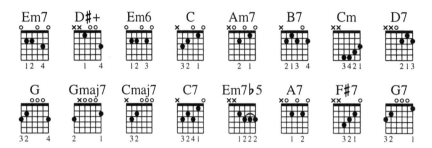

Strum Pattern: 4
Pick Pattern: 5

Moderately

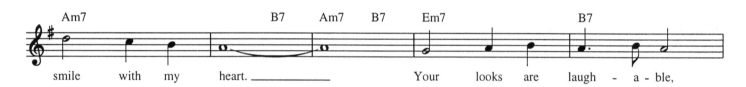

My fun-ny val-en-tine, sweet com-ic val-en-tine, you make me

smile with my heart. _____ Your looks are laugh-a-ble,

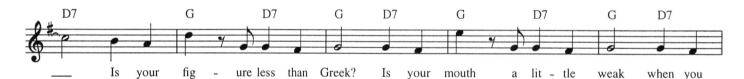

un-pho-to-graph-a-ble, yet, you're my fav-'rite work of art. _____

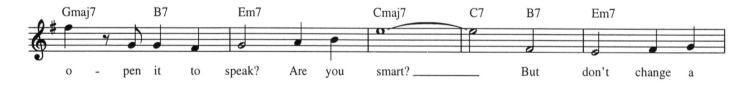

___ Is your fig-ure less than Greek? Is your mouth a lit-tle weak when you

o-pen it to speak? Are you smart? _____ But don't change a

hair for me, not if you care for me, stay lit-tle val-en-tine,

stay! _____ Each day is Val-en-tine's Day. _____

New Kid in Town

Words and Music by John David Souther, Don Henley and Glenn Frey

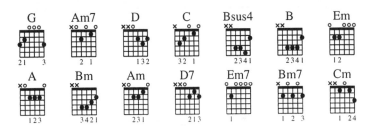

Strum Pattern: 3, 6
Pick Pattern: 3, 5

Intro
Moderately

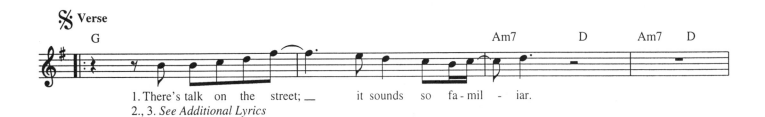

1. There's talk on the street; __ it sounds so fa-mil-iar.
2., 3. *See Additional Lyrics*

Great ex-pec-ta - tions, ev-'ry-bod - y's watch-ing you. __

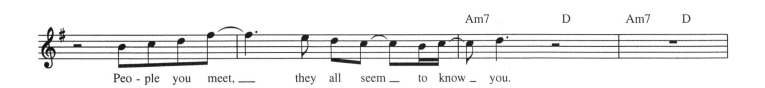

Peo - ple you meet, __ they all seem __ to know __ you.

E - ven your old _____ friends treat you like you're some-thing new. __

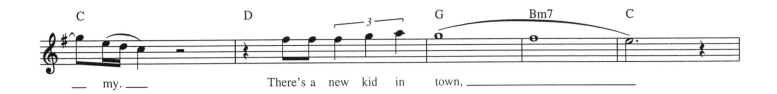

_ my. _   There's a new kid in town, _____

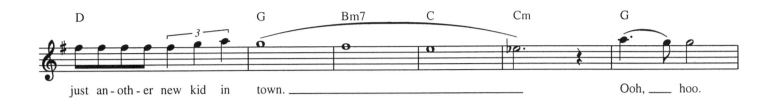

just an-oth-er new kid in town. _____ Ooh, ____ hoo.

Ev - 'ry - bod - y's talk - ing 'bout the new kid in town.   Ooh, _____ hoo.

Ev - 'ry - bod - y's walk - ing like the new kid in town.   There's a new kid in town.

I don't want to hear it. There's a new kid in town.   I ____ don't want to hear it. There's a

Outro   *Repeat and Fade*

new kid in town.   There's a new kid in town.   There's a

Additional Lyrics

2. You look in her eyes; the music begins to play.
   Hopeless romantics, here we go again.
   But after awhile you're looking the other way.
   It's those restless hearts that never mend.

3. There's talk on the street; it's there to remind you
   That it doesn't really matter which side you're on.
   You're walking away and they're talking behind you.
   They will never forget you till somebody new comes along.

The Rainbow Connection

from THE MUPPET MOVIE

Words and Music by Paul Williams and Kenneth L. Ascher

Strum Pattern: 8, 9
Pick Pattern: 8, 9

Additional Lyrics

2. Who said that ev'ry wish could be heard and answered
When wished on the morning star?
Somebody thought of that, and someone believed it;
Look what it's done so far.

3. Have you been half asleep and have you heard voices?
I've heard them calling my name.
Is this the sweet sound that calls the young sailors?
The voice might be one and the same.

Take the "A" Train

Words and Music by Billy Strayhorn

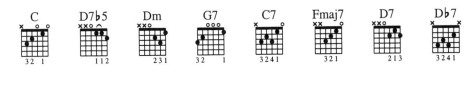

Strum Pattern: 3
Pick Pattern: 3

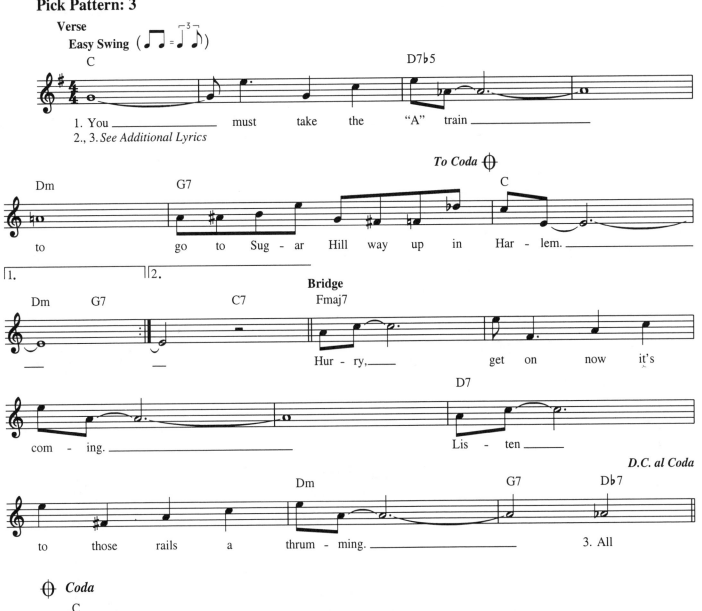

Additional Lyrics

2. If you miss the "A" train
   You'll find you've missed the quickest way to Harlem.

3. All 'board! Get on the "A" train.
   Soon you'll be on Sugar Hill in Harlem.

Tennessee Flat Top Box

Words and Music by Johnny Cash

Strum Pattern: 2
Pick Pattern: 4

Time

Words and Music by Roger Waters, Nicholas Mason, David Gilmour and Rick Wright

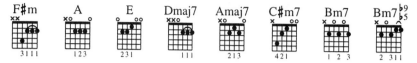

Strum Pattern: 6
Pick Pattern: 5

Verse
Moderately

1. Tick - ing a - way ___ the mo - ments that make up a dull ___ day;
2. *See Additional Lyrics*

frit - ter and waste ___ the hours ___ in an off - hand way. ___

Kick - ing a - round ___ on a piece of ground ___ in your home town;

wait - ing for some - one or some - thing to show ___ you the way. ___

Chorus
Half-Time Feel

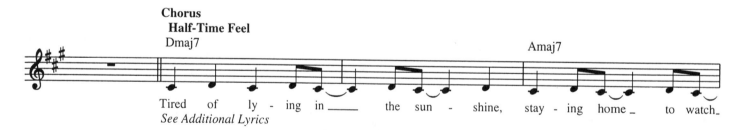

Tired of ly - ing in ___ the sun - shine, stay - ing home ___ to watch ___
See Additional Lyrics

___ the rain, you are young and life ___ is long, and there is time to kill ___

___ to - day. And then one day, you find ___ ten years have got

To Coda ⊕

Bm7 ... E

be-hind __ you. No one told you when __ to run. __ You missed the start-

Guitar Solo
End Half-Time Feel

F#m ... A ... E

- ing gun. _____

Half-Time Feel

F#m ... Dmaj7 ... Amaj7

play 4 times

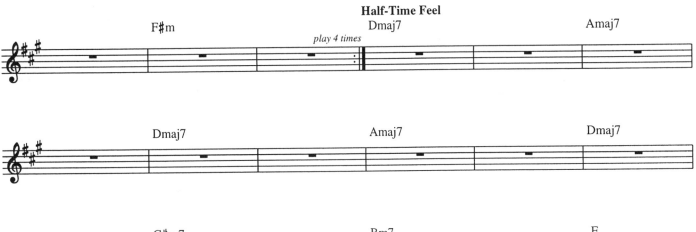

Dmaj7 ... Amaj7 ... Dmaj7

C#m7 ... Bm7 ... E

D.C. al Coda
End Half-Time Feel

2. And you

⊕ *Coda*

Bm7♭9♭5

Thought I'd some-thing more to say. _____

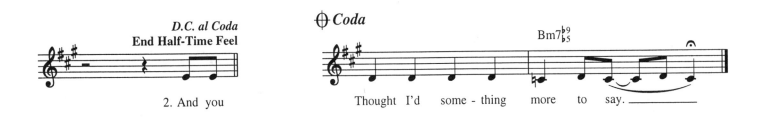

Additional Lyrics

2. And you run and you run to catch up with the sun, but it's sinking;
Racing around to come up behind you again.
The sun is the same in a relative way, but you're older.
Shorter of breath and one day closer to death.

Chorus Ev'ry year is getting shorter, never seem to find the time.
Plans that either come to naught or half a page of scribbled lines.
Hanging on in quiet desperation is the English way.
The time is gone. The song is over.
Thought I'd something more to say.

Tomorrow

from the Musical Production ANNIE

Lyric by Martin Charnin
Music by Charles Strouse

Strum Pattern: 1
Pick Pattern: 2

Moderately Slow

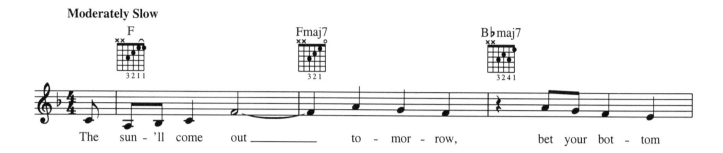

The sun – 'll come out _____ to - mor - row, bet your bot - tom

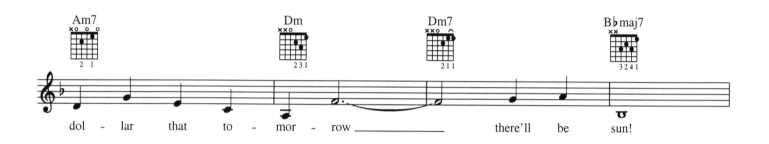

dol - lar that to - mor - row _____ there'll be sun!

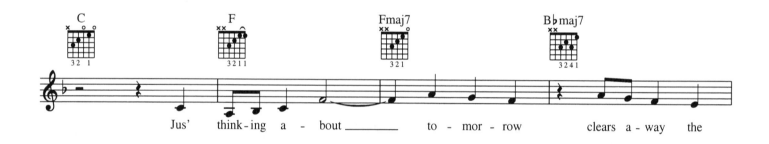

Jus' think - ing a - bout _____ to - mor - row clears a - way the

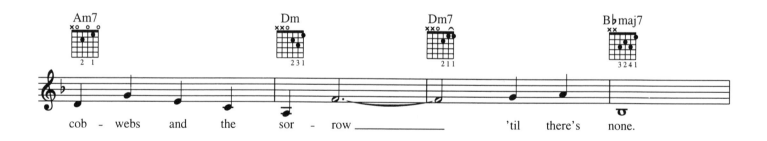

cob - webs and the sor - row _____ 'til there's none.

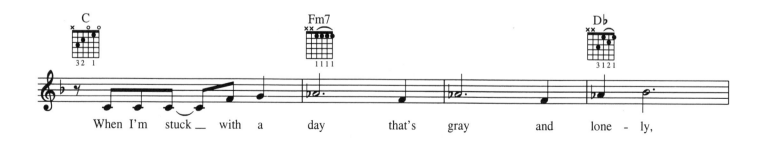

When I'm stuck __ with a day that's gray and lone - ly,

We Wish You a Merry Christmas

Traditional English Folksong

Strum Pattern: 8, 9
Pick Pattern: 8, 9

Additional Lyrics

2. We all know that Santa's coming.
   We all know that Santa's coming.
   We all know that Santa's coming
   And soon will be here.

Young Americans

Words and Music by David Bowie

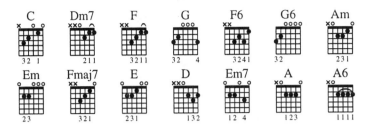

Strum Pattern: 3
Pick Pattern: 3

1. They pulled in just be-hind the fridge, _ he lays her down. _ He frowns, _

"Gee, my life's a fun - ny thing. Am I _____ still too young?"

He kissed her then and there; _ she took his ring, _ took his ba - bies. It

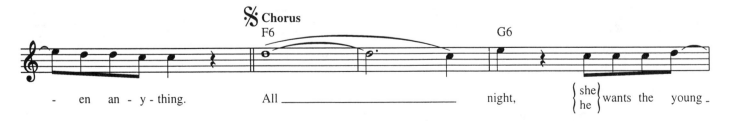

took him min - utes, took her no - where. _ Heav - en knows, _ she'd have tak-

-en an - y - thing. All _____ night, { she } { he } wants the young _

193

What I Like About You

Words and Music by Michael Skill, Wally Palamarchuk and James Marinos

Strum Pattern: 3
Pick Pattern: 3

Intro
Bright Rock

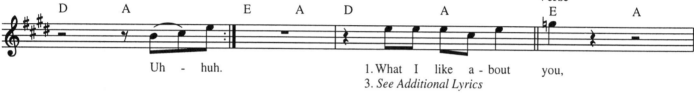

Hey!

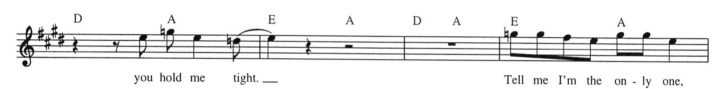

Uh - huh.

1. What I like a - bout you,
3. *See Additional Lyrics*

you hold me tight. ___ Tell me I'm the on - ly one,

wan - na come o - ver to - night. ___ Yeah! ___

Chorus

Keep on whis - per - ing in my ear, tell me all the things that I ___

___ wan - na hear, ___ 'cause it's true. ___ That's what I like a - bout

To Coda ⊕

Verse

you. 2. What I like a - bout you, you real - ly know how to dance. ___

Additional Lyrics

3. What I like about you,
   You keep me warm at night.
   Never wanna let you go,
   Know you make me feel alright. Yeah!

You're My Best Friend

Words and Music by John Deacon

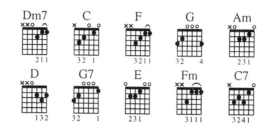

Strum Pattern: 3
Pick Pattern: 3

Intro
Moderately

1. Ooh, you make me live. _
2. *See Additional Lyrics*

What - ev - er this world can give to me. _ It's you, you're all I ___ see. _

___ Ooh, you make me live ___ now, hon - ey. Ooh, you make me live. _

___ Ooh, ___ you're the best ___ friend ___ that I _____ ev - er had. _ I've

been with you such a long time. ___ You're my sun - shine ___ and I want _

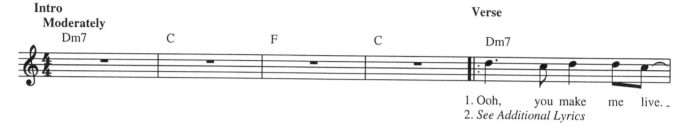

___ you to know _ that my feel - ings are true. _ I real - ly love you.

*Use Pattern 10

Oh, ___ you're my best ___ friend. ___ Ooh, you make me live. ___

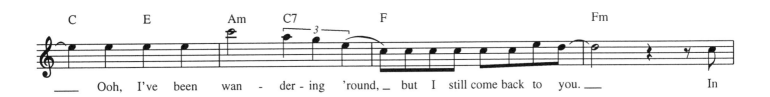

___ Ooh, I've been wan - der - ing 'round, _ but I still come back to you. ___ In

rain or shine ___ you've stood by me, girl, _ I'm hap - py at home, _ you're my best _

___ friend. _ Ooh, ooh, ___ you're my best _

___ friend. _ Ooh, you make me live. ___ Ooh, you're my best friend. _

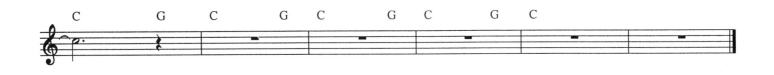

Additional Lyrics

2. Ooh, you make me live.
   Whenever this world is cruel to me.
   I got you to help me forgive.
   Ooh, you make me live now, honey.
   Ooh, you make me live.
   Ooh, you're the first one when things turn out bad.
   You know I'll never be lonely, you're my only one.
   And I love the things, I really love the things that you do.
   Oh, you're my best friend.

When Sunny Gets Blue

Lyric by Jack Segal
Music by Marvin Fisher

I Could Write a Book

from PAL JOEY

Words by Lorenz Hart

Music by Richard Rodgers

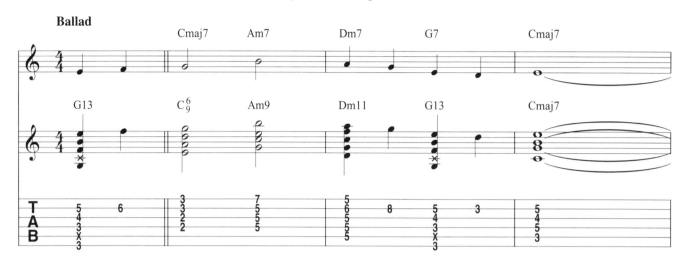

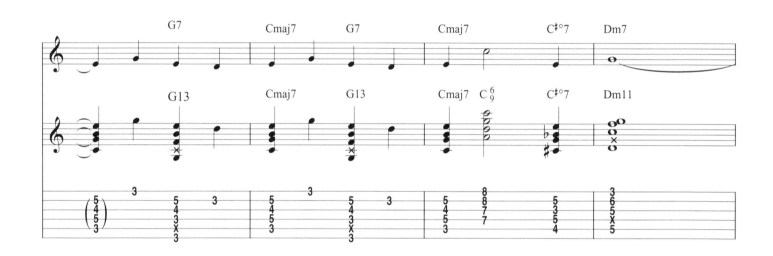

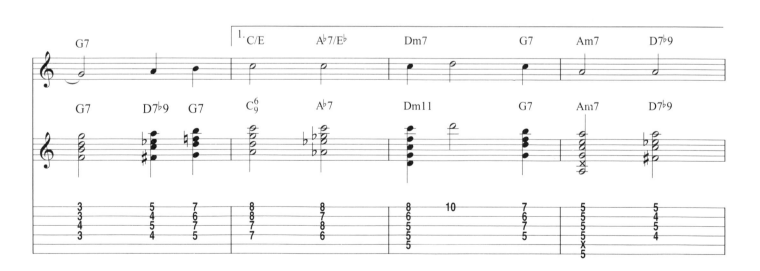

When I Fall in Love

Words by Edward Heyman
Music by Victor Young

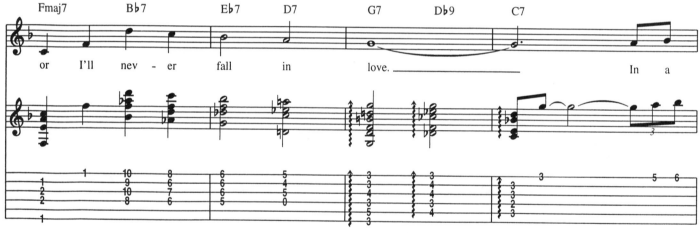

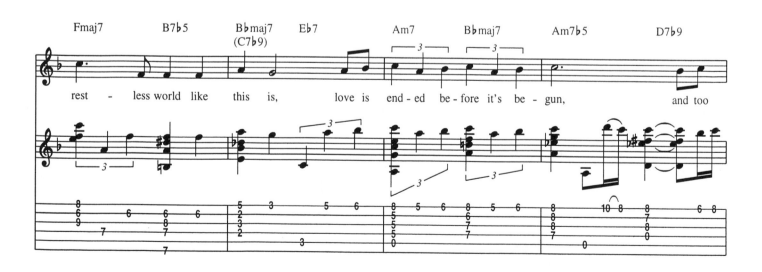

Andantino

By Mauro Giuseppe Sergio Pantaleo Giuliani

Prelude

Anonymous

Drop D tuning:
(low to high) D - A - D - G - B - E

Allegretto

By Fernando Carulli

Gavotte

By Lodovico Roncalli

Gigue

By Johann Anton Logy

Study in A Major
(Op. 6, No. 2)

By Fernando Sor

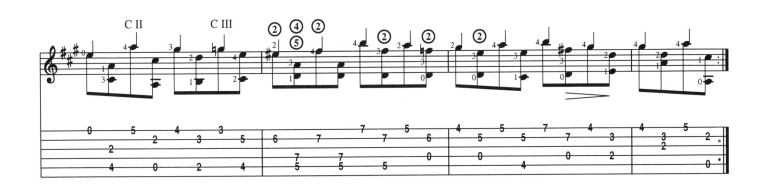

Study in A
(Op. 60, No. 3)

By Matteo Carcassi

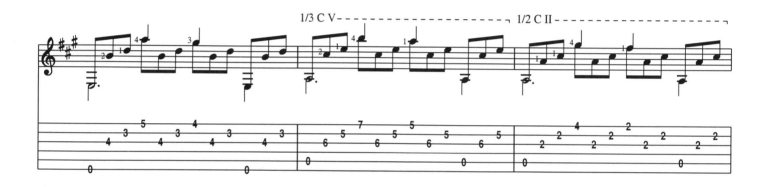

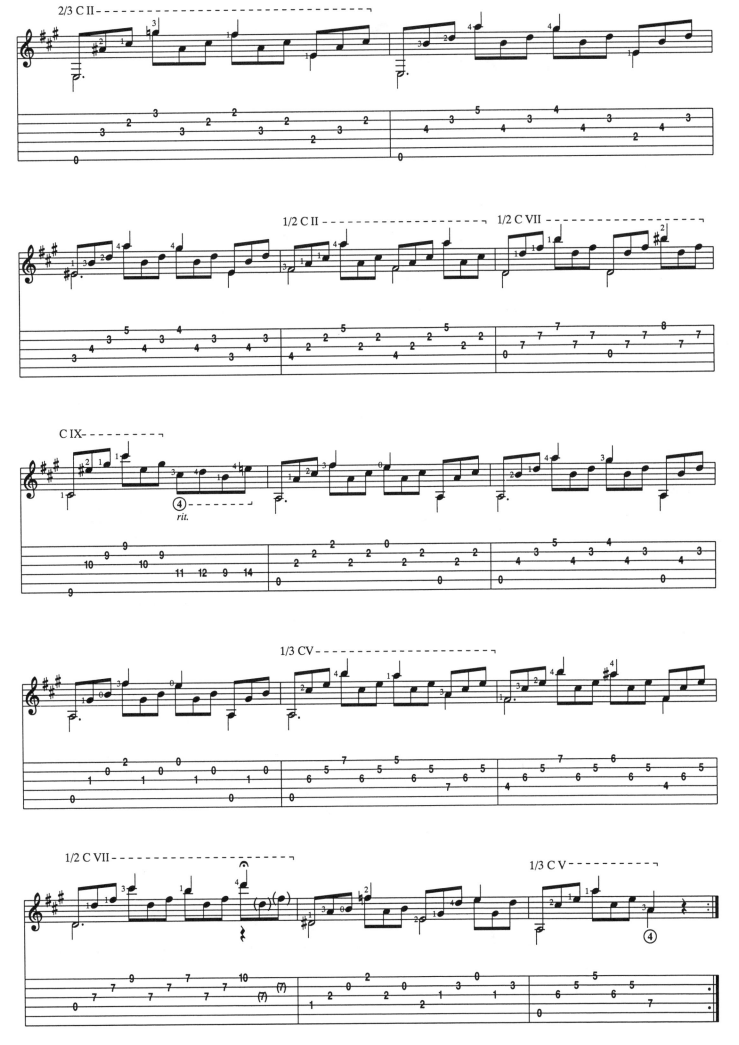

The Christmas Song
(Chestnuts Roasting on an Open Fire)

Music and Lyric by Mel Torme and Robert Wells

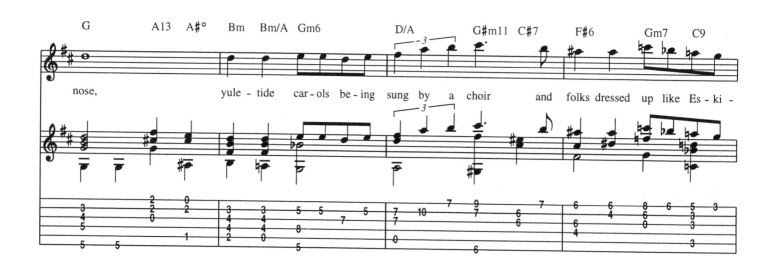

Imagine

Words and Music by John Lennon

a - bove us on - - ly sky. __
and no re - li - gion too. __
Im - ag - ine all the
Im - ag - ine all the

peo - ple
peo - ple
liv - ing
shar - ing
for
all
to - day. Ah. __
the world. You __

__ 2. Im - ag - ine there's no __ You may say __ I'm a

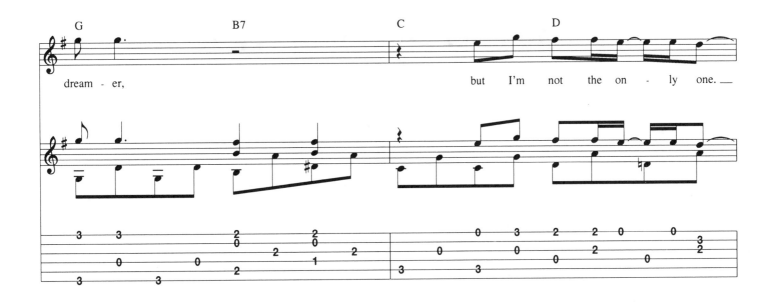

dream - er, but I'm not the on - ly one. ___

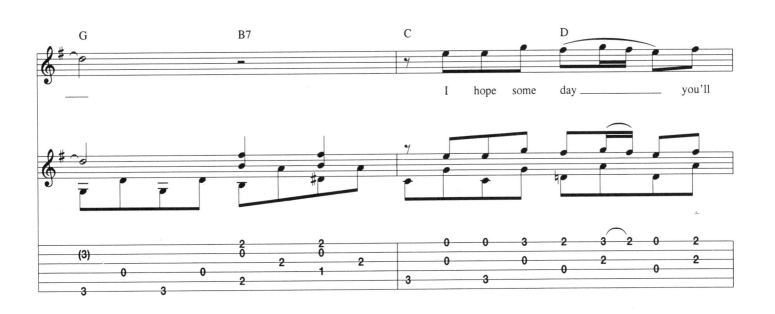

___ I hope some day _____ you'll

join us and the world _____ will live as one.

My One and Only Love

Words by Robert Mellin
Music by Guy Wood

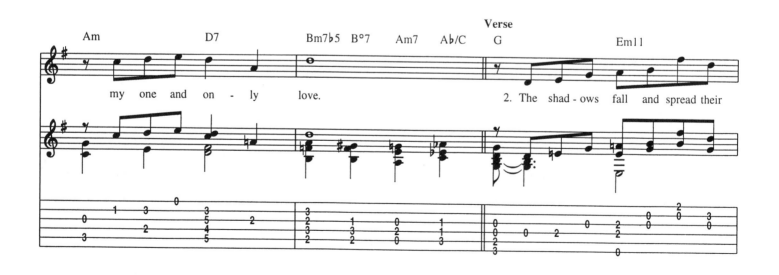

Where Do I Begin
(Love Theme)

from the Paramount Picture LOVE STORY

Words by Carl Sigman
Music by Francis Lai

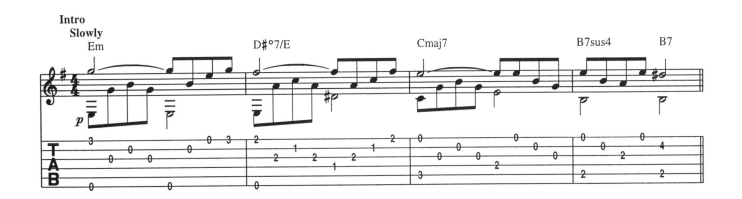

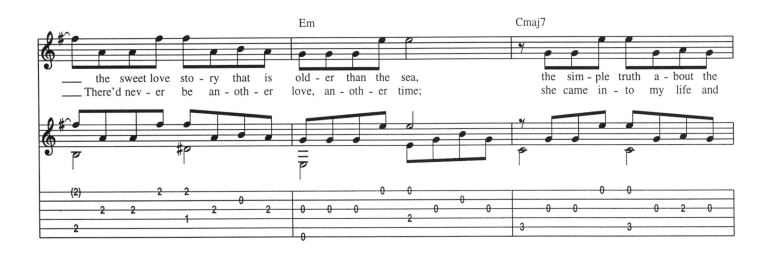

Outro

You Needed Me

Words and Music by Randy Goodrum

℠ Verse

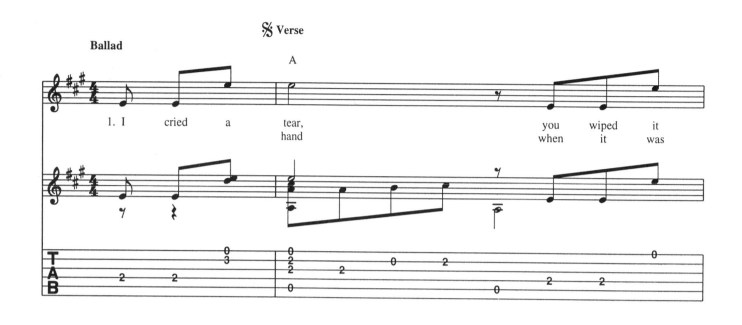

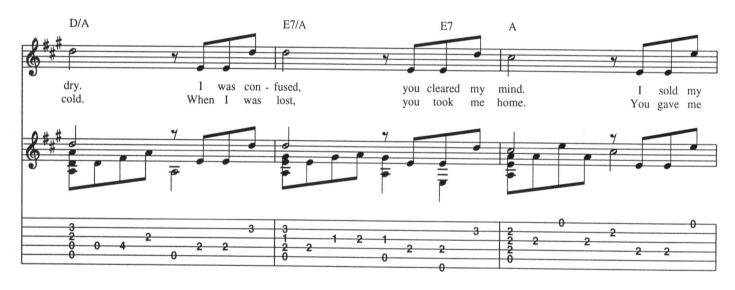

dig - ni - ty.   Some - how you need - ed me.
truth a - gain.   You e - ven called me friend.

You gave me strength   to stand a -

Chorus

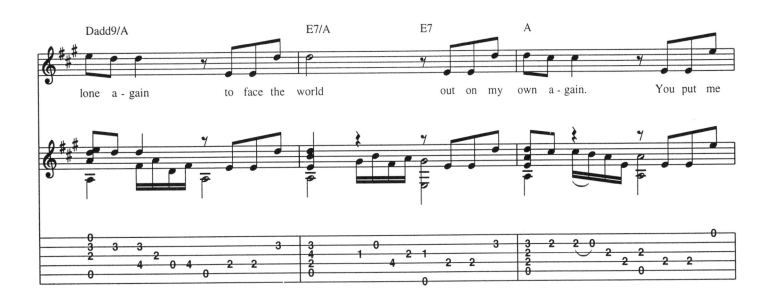

lone a - gain   to face the world   out on my own a - gain.   You put me

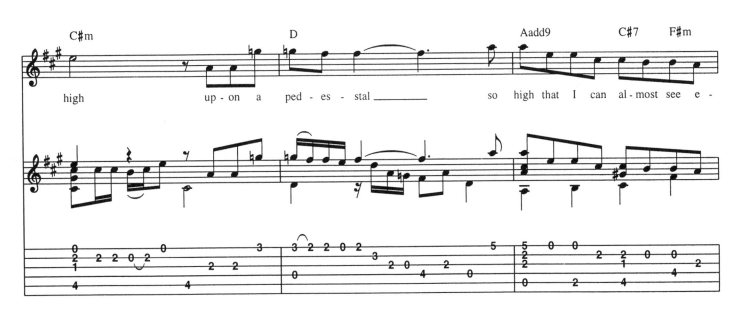

high   up - on a ped - es - stal _____ so high that I can al - most see e -

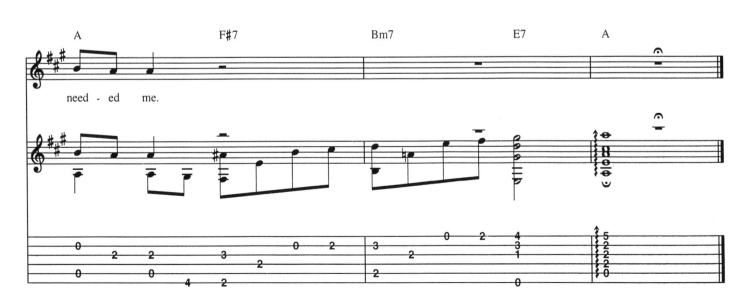

Call Me the Breeze

Words and Music by John Cale

Last Child

Words and Music by Steven Tyler and Brad Whitford

Rebel, Rebel

Words and Music by David Bowie

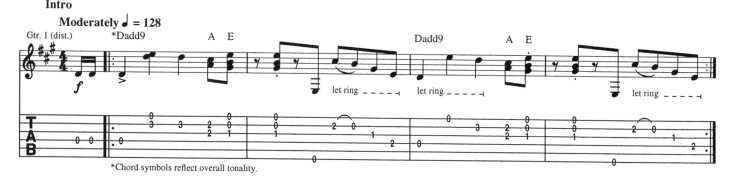

*Chord symbols reflect overall tonality.

Fire and Rain

Words and Music by James Taylor

Capo III

Intro
Moderately ♩ = 77

*Symbols in parentheses represent chord names respective to capoed guitar.
Symbols above reflect actual sounding chords. Capoed fret is "0" in TAB.

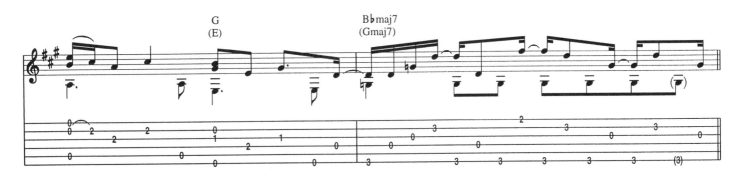

Green-Eyed Lady

Words and Music by Jerry Corbetta, J.C. Phillips and David Riordan

Intro
Gtr. 1
(clean)
Moderately Fast ♩ = 152

*Key signature denotes E Dorian.

Jessica

Words and Music by Dickey Betts

Intro
Uptempo Country Rock ♩ = 208

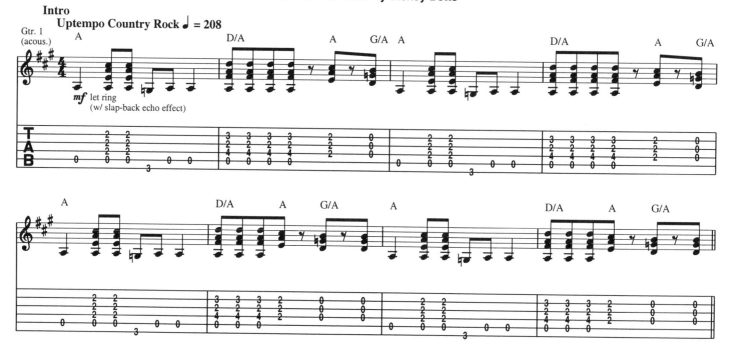

Maggie May

Words and Music by Rod Stewart and Martin Quittenton

Intro
Rubato (♩ = 130)

Rock and Roll Hoochie Koo

Words and Music by Rick Derringer

Shattered

Words and Music by Mick Jagger and Keith Richards

Stayin' Alive

from SATURDAY NIGHT FEVER

Words and Music by Barry Gibb, Maurice Gibb and Robin Gibb

Sweet Leaf

Words and Music by Frank Iommi, John Osbourne, William Ward and Terence Butler

Twist and Shout

Words and Music by Bert Russell and Phil Medley

You Were Meant for Me

Words and Music by Jewel Kilcher and Steve Poltz

STRUM AND PICK PATTERNS

This chart contains the suggested strum and pick patterns that are referred to by number at the beginning of each song in this book. The symbols ⊓ and ⋁ in the strum patterns refer to down and up strokes, respectively. The letters in the pick patterns indicate which right-hand fingers plays which strings.

p = thumb
i = index finger
m = middle finger
a = ring finger

For example; Pick Pattern 2
is played: thumb - index - middle - ring

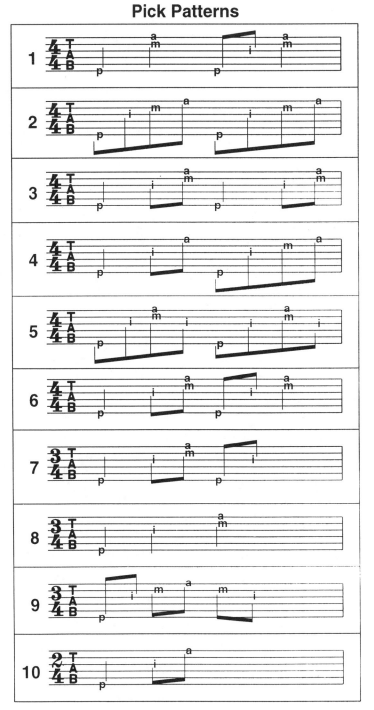

You can use the 3/4 Strum or Pick Patterns in songs written in compound meter (6/8, 9/8, 12/8, etc.). For example, you can accompany a song in 6/8 by playing the 3/4 pattern twice in each measure. The 4/4 Strum and Pick Patterns can be used for songs written in cut time (¢) by doubling the note time values in the patterns. Each pattern would therefore last two measures in cut time.

Guitar Notation Legend

Guitar Music can be notated three different ways: on a *musical staff*, in *tablature*, and in *rhythm slashes*.

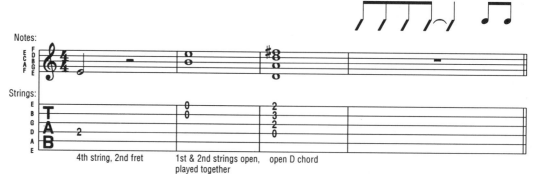

RHYTHM SLASHES are written above the staff. Strum chords in the rhythm indicated. Use the chord diagrams found at the top of the first page of the transcription for the appropriate chord voicings. Round noteheads indicate single notes.

THE MUSICAL STAFF shows pitches and rhythms and is divided by bar lines into measures. Pitches are named after the first seven letters of the alphabet.

TABLATURE graphically represents the guitar fingerboard. Each horizontal line represents a string, and each number represents a fret.

4th string, 2nd fret   1st & 2nd strings open,   open D chord
played together

HALF-STEP BEND: Strike the note and bend up 1/2 step.

WHOLE-STEP BEND: Strike the note and bend up one step.

GRACE NOTE BEND: Strike the note and bend up as indicated. The first note does not take up any time.

SLIGHT (MICROTONE) BEND: Strike the note and bend up 1/4 step.

BEND AND RELEASE: Strike the note and bend up as indicated, then release back to the original note. Only the first note is struck.

PRE-BEND: Bend the note as indicated, then strike it.

VIBRATO: The string is vibrated by rapidly bending and releasing the note with the fretting hand.

WIDE VIBRATO: The pitch is varied to a greater degree by vibrating with the fretting hand.

HAMMER-ON: Strike the first (lower) note with one finger, then sound the higher note (on the same string) with another finger by fretting it without picking.

PULL-OFF: Place both fingers on the notes to be sounded. Strike the first note and without picking, pull the finger off to sound the second (lower) note.

LEGATO SLIDE: Strike the first note and then slide the same fret-hand finger up or down to the second note. The second note is not struck.

SHIFT SLIDE: Same as legato slide, except the second note is struck.

TRILL: Very rapidly alternate between the notes indicated by continuously hammering on and pulling off.

TAPPING: Hammer ("tap") the fret indicated with the pick-hand index or middle finger and pull off to the note fretted by the fret hand.

NATURAL HARMONIC: Strike the note while the fret-hand lightly touches the string directly over the fret indicated.

PINCH HARMONIC: The note is fretted normally and a harmonic is produced by adding the edge of the thumb or the tip of the index finger of the pick hand to the normal pick attack.

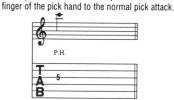

PICK SCRAPE: The edge of the pick is rubbed down (or up) the string, producing a scratchy sound.

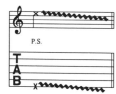

MUFFLED STRINGS: A percussive sound is produced by laying the fret hand across the string(s) without depressing, and striking them with the pick hand.

PALM MUTING: The note is partially muted by the pick hand lightly touching the string(s) just before the bridge.

RAKE: Drag the pick across the strings indicated with a single motion.

TREMOLO PICKING: The note is picked as rapidly and continuously as possible.

VIBRATO BAR DIVE AND RETURN: The pitch of the note or chord is dropped a specified number of steps (in rhythm) then returned to the original pitch.

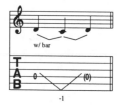

VIBRATO BAR SCOOP: Depress the bar just before striking the note, then quickly release the bar.

VIBRATO BAR DIP: Strike the note and then immediately drop a specified number of steps, then release back to the original pitch.